"Leadership," as the ⟨...⟩ "is the most studied a⟨...⟩ the social sciences." T⟨...⟩ discipline hasn't deter⟨...⟩ ⟨...⟩, redundant flood of literature on the topic, and much of it merely underscores his humble admission. In *The Sound of Leadership*, the seasoned leader Jules Glanzer achieves the sonorous outcome of *saying something new*. His voice will resonate with leaders who hearken for a deeper understanding of their art.

—**Joseph Castleberry**, Ed.D., President,
Northwest University

This book approaches leadership as a musical score, as art rather than science, as an orientation rather than a collection of tips, tricks, or tools. It's the self-reflective voice of a leader whose insights are grounded in the crucible of real experience. This book will show those who are considering leadership roles what's involved. It will help new leaders understand how to approach the challenges they will encounter. Those who are already responsible for guiding groups and organizations will be encouraged to reflect on, and fine tune their own approaches to leadership. The anecdotes from real life not only illustrate the principles being presented but also make for a very interesting read!

—**D. Merrill Ewert**, Ph.D., President Emeritus,
Fresno Pacific University

Jesus said, "My sheep listen to my voice; I know them, and they follow me" (John 10:27). Jules Glanzer's book, *The Sound of Leadership*, strikes an essential note regarding Kingdom leadership: it is like sound. Sound is relational. It requires someone to make it and someone to receive it. Kingdom leaders hear and follow the King - and they in turn invite others to do the same. Dr. Glanzer's book has a dual effect of tuning out the cacophonous voices that disorient us while reorienting us to the One Voice that calls us by name.

—**Charles J. Conniry, Jr.**, Ph.D., President,
Western Seminary

Informed by Scripture and shaped by insights and wisdom from years of valuable leadership experience, Jules Glanzer has provided a gift for seasoned leaders, newer leaders, and those looking for leadership opportunities. Glanzer emphasizes the importance of bringing diverse people together around a unifying mission and vision. He thoughtfully exhorts leaders not only to care for others, but to care for themselves through the faithful practice of the spiritual disciplines. *The Sound of Leadership* encourages readers to develop the gifts of discernment, listening well, wise decision making, and an ever-present trust in the Lord for all aspects of life and service. It is a genuine joy to enthusiastically recommend this fine work from Jules Glanzer.

—**David S. Dockery**, President, International Alliance for Christian Education and Distinguished Professor of Theology, Southwestern Baptist Theological Seminary

The book title Sound of Leadership sounds interesting to a guy who is intrigued by both music and leadership. The Beatles, the Eagles, the Beachboys, Chicago, some of Handel's and Buxtehude's and Rachmaninoff's works, and Matt Redmond for sure.

While there is considerable ado about music stuff, readers may find the most satisfying content in Glanzer's blending of personal insights with those of several authors from the leadership genre. Scores of helpful leadership notes harmonize well with strong scriptural undertones. It is encouraging to be reminded that every leader is unique, but that there will be a common unison of integrity among them. Vocalists are coached to sing their stories with passion. Glanzer's solo is both comprehendible and commendable.

The takeaway prompts and other evaluation prods will be useful for those who want to digest the primary insights and put them into practice.

—**Ed Boschman**, D. Min., Church Consultant and Certified Life Coach

The topic of leadership is among the most popular of all written material. In this book, Jules has brought together the strands of his personal life, his experience of leading institutions, Biblical principles of leadership that have stood the test of time, and music to create a book of interest and content that are worth the read.

> —**Larry Nikkel**, CEO Prairie View Hospital and Mental Health Center, CEO Mennonite Health Services

Reading *The Sound of Leadership*, I felt like I was with Jules at his home, with a cup of good coffee, talking about leadership. He brings together his knowledge of people, his experience in leadership, and his understanding of our Scriptures to weave a cloth that shows a fresh look at leadership for followers of Jesus. Using the analogy of leadership to compare it with a complicated piece of music, Jules focuses on the role of the conductor (leader) in presenting a beautiful concert (successful organization). I particularly like how this book gives a "big picture" look at successful leadership.

> —**H. David Brandt**, President Emeritus, George Fox University

I first came to know Dr. Jules Glanzer in the late 1970s as my pastor in a small but thriving church in southwest Kansas. Over the years our lives intersected at infrequent times and then more so when Jules became President of Tabor College. As a denominational leader, I find Jules's book, *The Sound of Leadership* to be a deeply rich and helpful read for myself and in my view, for leaders in all capacities. Using words that infiltrate the music world for expanding ideas and principles for leadership brought a fresh, invigorating, and piercing look into the vital aspects of good leadership. I gleaned many new thoughts and usable direction from this book, which with the plethora of books on leadership I currently have on my shelves, is rather unusual. This is a book worth reading...slowly. And with one's heart open to hear the music.

> —**Don Morris**, USMB National Director

Just as there are many styles of music, scholars and practitioners have devised many ways to discuss the topic of leadership. In *The Sound of Leadership*, Dr. Glanzer has skillfully arranged his personal leadership experiences into a soundtrack of applicable principles for readers to put into practice. Those who choose to listen to *The Sound of Leadership* will be uplifted by the refrain of Dr. Glanzer›s faith woven into this story.

—**Norm Duncan**, Ph.D. in Leadership

If you really care about effective leadership that fulfils the call of Jesus Christ to "seek first the Kingdom of God" in all of life, and especially if you long for such leadership in every earthly organization that you care about, including your church, then you need this book. There are countless leadership books that are much longer, more complicated, often obtuse, or even self-contradictory, and that still miss key elements of organizational leadership. This book is compact, clear, complete, and, like great music, it is beautifully moving. You can trust this Spirit-led and biblically grounded wisdom to guide and inspire organizations that demonstrate the character of the Kingdom of God. As a bonus, this book provides an excellent framework for your followership role of choosing, supporting, and evaluating those who lead.

—**Richard Kriegbaum**, Ph.D., President Emeritus, Fresno Pacific University

This wonderful little book zeroes in on the person of the leader rather than, as is common, on the techniques of leadership. Building on the biblical insight that it is the Divine Sound that has brought all things into being, Jules Glanzer demonstrates that it is also the sound created by the leader that now helps shape the Divine Kingdom. Those who disparage the intrinsic role of faith in shaping leadership may find Glanzer's avowedly pervasive faith perspective off-putting. Leaders of faith, however, will almost certainly find Glanzer's insights truly inspiring.

—**Carl E. Zylstra**, Ph.D., President Emeritus Dordt University

invite PRESS

THE SOUND OF LEADERSHIP

Jules Glanzer
Foreword by Leonard Sweet

THE SOUND OF LEADERSHIP

Kingdom Notes to Fine Tune
Your Life and Influence

invite PRESS
Plano, Texas

**The Sound of Leadership:
Kingdom Notes to Fine Tune Your Life and Influence**

Copyright 2023 by Jules Glanzer

All rights reserved.

No part of this work may be reproduced or transmitted in any form or by any means, electronic or mechanical, including photocopying and recording, or by any information storage or retrieval system, except as may be expressly permitted by the 1976 Copyright Act or in writing from the publisher. Requests for permission can be addressed to Permissions, Invite Press, P.O. Box 260917, Plano, TX 75026.

This book is printed on acid-free, elemental chlorine-free paper.

ISBN 978-1-953495-62-4; epub 978-1-953495-63-1

All scripture quotations unless noted otherwise are taken from THE HOLY BIBLE, NEW INTERNATIONAL VERSION®, NIV® Copyright © 1973, 1978, 1984, 2011 by Biblica, Inc.™ Used by permission of Zondervan. All rights reserved worldwide.

Scripture quotations marked NLT are taken from Holy Bible, New Living Translation, copyright © 1996, 2004, 2015 by Tyndale House Foundation. Used by permission of Tyndale House Publishers, Inc., Carol Stream, Illinois 60188. All rights reserved.

Scripture quotations marked KJV are taken from the King James Version (public domain).

Scripture quotations marked (THE MESSAGE) are taken from THE MESSAGE, Copyright © by Eugene H. Peterson 1993, 1994, 1995, 1996, 2000, 2001, 2002. Used be permission of NavPress Publishing Group.

23 24 25 26 27 28 29 30 31 32—10 9 8 7 6 5 4 3 2 1

MANUFACTURED IN THE UNITED STATES OF AMERICA

DEDICATION

To the voices who have spoken into my life and leadership over the years:

Marvin Sellberg, whose voice taught me business and economics, which I have used my entire life

Henry Schmidt, whose voice shaped my understanding of ministry and influenced me throughout life

Leonard Sweet, whose voice shaped how I lead by the sound of his thinking, writing, and friendship

Richard Kriegbaum, whose voice provided wisdom while serving in Christian higher education

Pat McLaughlin, whose voice created the legacy of my presidency

Grandma Mendel, whose voice still touches my soul after all these years

Peg, whose voice is always present

CONTENTS

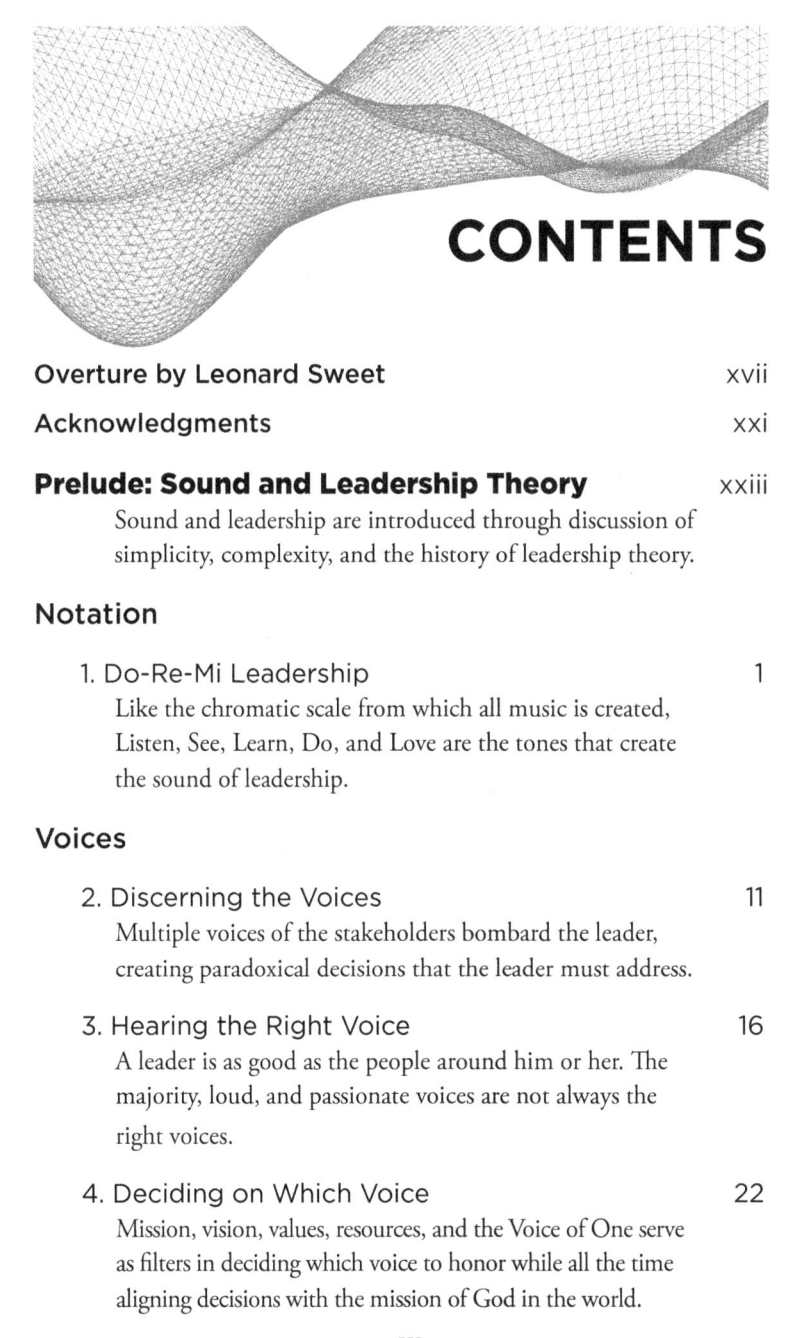

Overture by Leonard Sweet   xvii

Acknowledgments   xxi

Prelude: Sound and Leadership Theory   xxiii
    Sound and leadership are introduced through discussion of simplicity, complexity, and the history of leadership theory.

Notation

    1. Do-Re-Mi Leadership   1
        Like the chromatic scale from which all music is created, Listen, See, Learn, Do, and Love are the tones that create the sound of leadership.

Voices

    2. Discerning the Voices   11
        Multiple voices of the stakeholders bombard the leader, creating paradoxical decisions that the leader must address.

    3. Hearing the Right Voice   16
        A leader is as good as the people around him or her. The majority, loud, and passionate voices are not always the right voices.

    4. Deciding on Which Voice   22
        Mission, vision, values, resources, and the Voice of One serve as filters in deciding which voice to honor while all the time aligning decisions with the mission of God in the world.

5. Listening to the Voice of One   29
Jesus is our model for listening to the Voice of One.

Interlude Music and Leadership   37

Music

6. Enrolling in God's School of Music   39
God calls, prepares, and creates masterpieces from the experiences of our lives. Our sovereign foundations, inner-life growth, ministry and life maturing experiences, all prepare us by converging for such a time as this.

7. Composing Your Song   45
Leadership is being that results in doing. Integrity of heart and skillful hands are part of the song we compose as leaders. Integrity, courage, and humility are character qualities that create a harmonious song.

8. Playing Your Song   51
Your persona and style become the voice, tone, and mood of your leadership. How you treat people is the song you play. Practicing the golden rule and living by the gold standard of excellence is the music people hear when you lead.

9. Dancing to the Music   57
Celebrating accomplishments and demonstrating leadership service attitudes and actions of gratefulness, generosity, and graciousness lead to a life well lived.

10. Choosing Your Genre   64
The legacy a leader desires, the legacy the situation will dictate, and the legacy assigned to the leader by his or her actions and attitudes are like a genre ascribed to a leader. The legacy a leader leaves will fade. The legacy a leader lives will continue.

11. Harmonizing the Voices   71
Aligning a team to live up to the expectation to speak the truth in love, embrace hard realities, entrust responsibilities, and require loyalty creates a harmonious sound. Creativity and innovation enhance the harmony.

12. Songbook of Leadership — 79
The Psalms provide us with a theology of leadership that becomes the score for our compositions.

Interlude Noise (Sound Variations) and Leadership — 89

Noise

13. Sound Frequencies — 91
Leadership in the kingdom is measured differently than natural leadership.

14. Sound Waves — 98
Discover your destiny as a leader by doing a case study on yourself.

15. Sound Effects — 107
Replace blaming, complaining, and defending with taking responsibility, recognizing that decisions have consequences, and learning from failure.

16. Sound of Silence — 113
Lead from a divine center by practicing the disciplines of solitude, silence, and guided prayer.

Postlude: Creating a Magnum Opus — 117

A leader's magnum opus is influencing and developing more leaders. Leadership development begins with ideas, requires reflection, involves participation, needs relationship, and is best expressed in entrepreneurship and service.

Reprise: Sovereign Leadership Lessons from COVID-19 — 125

We serve at the pleasure of the Lord. Our responsibility is to trust him.

Appendix A — 129
Appendix B — 131
Endnotes — 133

OVERTURE
By Leonard Sweet

Music is liquid architecture;
architecture is frozen music.
Johann Wolfgang von Goethe (1749–1832)

"If you want to find the secrets of the universe, think in terms of energy, frequency, and vibration," prophesied inventor and futurist Nikola Tesla (1856–1943). Albert Einstein (1879-1955) pushed Tesla's prophecy forward with what became the world's most famous formula, $E=mc^2$, which expressed mathematically that energy and matter are basically interchangeable. Superstring physicists have subsequently chimed in with their bottom-line definition of "matter" as "vibrating strings of energy."

Since energy, frequency, and vibration constitute the essence of sound, to inhabit the future we must reframe everything in terms of acoustics. Hence, matter isn't "matter." Matter doesn't "matter." Matter is music.

Jules Glanzer has started this reframing in his wise, witty, winsome book, *The Sound of Leadership*, in which the vocation of leadership is best seen as a musical score or an acoustical art. The vocation of leadership calls for sound artists. The word "vocation" shares with "vocal" the same root word, *vocare*, which is Latin for "calling" or "speaking," as in "God calling" or "God speaking." A college, a company, and a church are all acoustic communities that hear into speech and sight and body forth into action. Leadership is learning how to "read" the culture with both ears (in surround sound) and both eyes (while cross-eyed), the invisible first, then the visible, with our ears leading the way for all five-plus senses.

Britain's first "Professor of Radio," Séan Street,[1] in his book *The Sound of a Room*, asserts that a place takes on personality through its sounds. After attending worship at Lincoln Cathedral, Professor Street spoke of how the voices of the choir flowed in and out of the structure like liquid so that the song "was actually becoming the building."[2] "Sound memory," like smell, brings moments back to us; but unlike smell, sound memory, in a reciprocal and fluid fashion, takes us back "there," while we are still *here*. Street's entire book is an endorsement of one of the major finds of cognitive neuroscience, which studies relationships between thought processes and brain functions. The essential gift of humanity is our ability to attach complex meanings to sounds.

Archaeoacoustics is a new discipline yoking archaeology and acoustics. It focuses on the relationship between people and sound throughout history. In many ways we are only catching up to our ancestors, such as the translators of the King James Bible. Part of the enduring attachment of the ages to the 1611 Authorized Version is the mellifluous sonority of its words. The forty-seven scholars who translated the Hebrew and Greek into English would meet periodically to read their translations to one another. They intuited that to get the meaning of the words right, they also had to get the sound of the words right. The King James Bible was translated from the sound up. This may be true of more classic works of literature than we know. Playwright Arthur Miller, author of *Death of a Salesman* (1949) remarked of his play-writing days, "I used to wear out my voice when I wrote."[3]

Archaeologists are finding more and more ancient cities that were built according to acoustic blueprints. Mayan temples are now understood as giant loudspeakers. Hal Saflieni Hypogeum, an underground necropolis in Malta, constructed around 3300–3000 BCE, features a series of subterranean chambers and catacomb temples all built to resonate at the same "holy frequency," 111 Hz. The grand structure was allegedly designed and tuned to hear sounds from the world beyond. A "niche" in the "Oracle Chamber" causes the human voice to echo throughout the entire structure. This has led some to believe that chanting was a key feature of prehistoric rituals.[4]

The Greek philosopher Pythagoras (570–490 BCE) created his musical scale starting with the note, A, which resonates at the frequency of 111 Hz, called the "Divine Frequency."[5] We know that 111 Hz is associated with healing and well-being through the production of endorphins, which assist in cell rejuvenation and regeneration. The sound relieves pain and elevates mood. Frequency 111 Hz can increase feelings of overall well-being and empathy and improve focus and memory. MRI scans show that this frequency affects the brain by switching off the prefrontal cortex, deactivating the language center, and inducing a meditative phase and pause. Scottish surgeon Dr. Meg Patterson worked on a therapy called NET based on treating different diseases by using frequencies. She reportedly helped the Who's Pete Townshend recover from heroin addiction using 111 Hz[6]. Perhaps eighteenth-century German mystic and Romantic philosopher Novalis was not deserving of scorn for saying, "Every sickness is a musical problem, and every cure is a musical solution."[7]

The primary metaphor for the Enlightenment and industrial world was either the machine or the billiard table. Everything was seen to work in clockwork fashion, with cause and effect the basis of all life. The primary metaphor for this twenty-first-century world is a musical symphony, consisting of rhythm, melody, and harmony. This is not a world based on balls or ball bearings but on notes, rhythm, sounds, and silences.

Jules Glanzer has written a profound book in easily accessible prose that readies the worlds of church, commerce, culture, and academe with a true lingua franca for leadership. Will there be a global language for the future? We already have one, as *The Sound of Leadership* demonstrates.

OVERTURE

It's a language that needs no translator or translation. It's a language the whole world speaks. It's the global staff of life:

Music and song.

Leonard Sweet
Author of 70+ books (e.g. Rings of Fire), Professor (Drew University, George Fox University, Northwind Seminary, Kairos), Publisher (The Salish Sea Press), and Founder of PreachTheStory.com

ACKNOWLEDGMENTS

I have written over a thousand speeches, dozens of strategic plans, many essays, a few articles, hundreds of letters, thousands of pages in a journal, a thesis and a dissertation. Writing a book is a whole different experience. When writing a book, you must have something to say, and unique to what has already been said. Book writing requires focus, discipline, and creativity. As an author, I want my ideas and words to cause people to think. I want the reader to go off on rabbit trails, remembering his or her own experiences and making application to his or her situations. I consider my writing successful when something I say stimulates the reader's imagination to go to new places in the mind. I attempt to meet that objective by saying less, saying it better, and not saying it all.

As a rookie author, I needed help in every aspect of the process toward becoming a published author. My thanks to . . .

> Len Wilson, for taking the risk with a no-name-no-platform author. His vision for publishing and his commitment to helping new authors are unique in the publishing world. May your tribe increase.

> Leonard Sweet, for writing a foreword and giving my voice credibility and exposure. His willingness to have his name associated with mine is humbling. The idea of leadership as an acoustical art and the power of images comes from him. I cherish our friendship.

Acknowledgments

Lori Wagner, for making the ideas and content into what my wife calls a "real book." Lori's positive encouragement, attention to detail, and grammatical and literary insights made it happen. Like a true leader, she equipped and inspired me along the way. Thank you.

Sheila Litke, who answered all my questions regarding music terminology and composition. Her advice and musical expertise kept me from looking ignorant. She continually demonstrates leadership service. Keep tickling the ivories.

Google. Seems silly to mention, but how does one write a book without the use of Google? Thank you, Larry Page and Sergei Brin. You and Johannes Gutenberg have a lot in common.

Invite Press staff. They know how to take the ideas of a South Dakota Hutterite farm boy and make them pleasing to the eye for anyone who wants to read about leadership. Thank you, Stephen Graham-Ching and Renee Chavez, for taking care of all the editing details. Thank you, Josiah Simons, Michael Buckingham, Lori Harmon, Kristen Shoates, Maurilio Amorim, and the entire A Group team for making my ideas sellable. As the saying goes, nothing happens until someone makes a sale.

PRELUDE
SOUND AND LEADERSHIP THEORY

*By the word of the L*ORD *the heavens were made,*
their starry host by the breath of his mouth. . . .
For he spoke, and it came to be;
he commanded, and it stood firm.

Psalm 33:6, 9

In the beginning God created the heavens and the earth. . . .
And God said, "Let there be light," and there was light.

Genesis 1:1, 3

Great leaders are almost always great simplifiers who can cut through the noise to offer a solution everybody can understand.

Gen. Colin Powell

A leader is one who, out of clutter, brings simplicity . . . out of discord, harmony . . . and out of difficult, opportunity.

Albert Einstein

Creation was a sound event. "And God said, 'Let there be . . .'" (Gen. 1:3, 6, 14). And there was. The existence of the universe came into being from a voice—the voice of God. In the same way, leadership is a sound experience. Leonard Sweet's definition of leadership is right-on: "Leadership is an acoustical art."[8] An effective leader can hear and discern the many voices while at the same time call other voices into a harmonious sound of imagining and creating the future. Simultaneously, one who has answered the call to bring together people to address a perceived need for the common good needs to develop his or her own personal soundtrack communicating a distinct voice and tone. All this is done under the umbrella of a firm conviction that the God who spoke the universe into existence still speaks today, fulfilling his mission in the world through people, whom he calls into leadership service and whom he equips and inspires to influence others toward his purposes.

Like creation, leadership embodies both simplicity and complexity. In its simplest form, leadership is influence. In its complex form, leadership is "stuck in the rut of trying harder and harder without obtaining significantly new results," all the time attempting to appease the many stakeholders of your organization.[9] Oliver Wendell Holmes once reputedly said, "I would not give a fig for the simplicity this side of complexity; but I would give my life for the simplicity the other side of complexity."[10] The purpose of this book is, through acoustical images, to present the simplicity of leadership on the other side of complexity with the hope that those who have been called into leadership service will lead diligently with smiles on their faces and joy in their hearts.

The science of sound is complex, complicated, and consequential. Defining it depends on the discipline in which you work. Sound can be described as a vibration (physics), a reception (physiology), a perception (psychology), a sensation (audiology), and a stimulation (music). The naked eye cannot see sound, only its effects.

Like sound, leadership is also complex, complicated, and consequential. It can be described in multiple ways depending on your frame of reference. A quick review of the history of leadership theory identifies numerous understandings of leadership. From the great man theory of the 1800s, the trait approaches of the early 1900s, the behavioral approaches of the mid-1900s, and situational approaches of the late 1900s, to the complexity era of the 1990s and 2000s and the current popular theory, called adaptive leadership, the evolution of leadership thinking continues. Influence that equips and inspires a group of people to go to a place they either could not or would not go by themselves is the essence of all leadership. Like sound, it cannot be seen, only experienced and its effects recognized. Using the three most recognizable sound images—voices, music, and noise—this book describes and explores basic leadership concepts and applies them to everyday leadership service.

I am convinced that everything revolves around leadership. Leadership matters. Practicing the acoustical art of leadership increases the effectiveness and enhances the outcomes of the person who has answered the call. Before one can see the future, learn about the situation, do what is required, and love those who have gathered, one must listen - to others and to the voice of God.

> **KINGDOM TAKEAWAY**
> In one simple sentence, state your understanding of leadership.

Sound: The Interface Between Heaven and Earth

Sound is the interface between heaven and earth.

The first event recorded in the scriptures is a sound event. "And *God said*, 'Let there be…'" (Genesis 1:3) And there was. The existence of the universe came into being from a voice… the voice of God. The final words of scripture are a sound invitation of the One who spoke creation into existence: "The Spirit and the bride say, 'Come!' And let the one *who hears* say, 'Come!'" (Revelation 22:17) Sandwiched between these sound events the scriptures record many significant events where the image of sound is mentioned.

When God gave the Ten Commandments, he was escorted with *thunder and a trumpet blast*. (Exodus 20:16) John the Baptist was known as "A *voice* of one calling in the wilderness." (Luke 3:4) At Jesus' baptism (Mark 1:11) and transfiguration (Matthew 17:5) they *heard a voice* from heaven. (Mark 1:11 & 9:7) Often the scriptures tell us that Jesus *spoke* when performing supernatural events. He "rebuked the wind and the waves." (Matthew 8:26) He told the paralyzed man to "Get up, take your mat and go home." (Matthew 9:6) He brought Lazarus back from the dead *shouting*, "Come out." (John 11:43) Parables are punctuated with "He who has *ears to hear…*" (Mark 4:23). Mary recognized Jesus at the empty tomb when he *spoke* her name. (John 21:17) The Holy Spirit's coming was like the "*sound* of a mighty rushing wind." (Act 2:2) Paul tells us that faith comes by *hearing* . . . (Romans 10:17). The entire visionary book of Revelation came to John in "a *loud voice* like a trumpet" telling him what to write. (Revelations 1:10, 4:1) And each of the letters to the seven churches in Revelation end with "Whoever has ears, *let them hear* . . ." (Revelation 2:7, 2:11, 2:17, 2:29 3:6, 3:13, 3:22)

Sound is the interface between heaven and earth.

NOTATION

CHAPTER ONE
DO-RE-MI LEADERSHIP

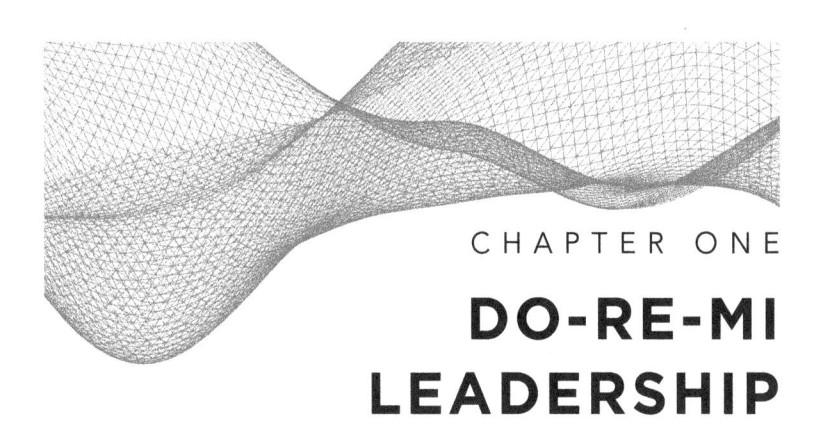

But seek first his kingdom and his righteousness, and all these things will be given to you as well.

Matthew 6:33

Lord, let your ear be attentive to the prayer of this your servant and to the prayer of your servants who delight in revering your name. Give your servant success today by granting him favor in the presence of this man.

Nehemiah 1:11

The best leaders, like the best music, inspire us to see new possibilities.
Max DePree, *Leadership Jazz*

Most of us learned the fundamentals of music theory in grade school music class by singing the song Julie Andrews made famous - "DO, a deer, a female deer," followed, as you will recall, by RE, MI, FA, SO, LA, TI and back to DO.

CHAPTER ONE

This diatonic scale of C D E F G A B C plus the chromatic scale, adding the sharps/flats, is central to all musical compositions. All music, harmonious or discordant, finds its source in these twelve notes. From "Chopsticks" to Beethoven's Ninth Symphony to Bruce Springsteen's "Born to Run," John Philip Sousa's "The Stars and Stripes Forever," or Eminem's "Lose Yourself," all are a variation of the tones from the chromatic scale. All music is a series of sound waves filling the air from these tones.

God-honoring, kingdom-seeking, biblically rooted leadership has a scale too. All the complexities of leadership, the required competencies and character, the convictions and courage to act, and the needed charisma and compassion to accomplish what is needed for the common good of the people fulfilling God's mission in the world, are built on five words:

Listen, See, Learn, Do, Love. These five words are the scale from which all leadership happens.

For leadership to happen, you need a situation that needs addressing, a group of people who desire to see a change, and a person prepared and called to bring them together for the common good. The biblical character Nehemiah was a great example. The walls of Jerusalem were in shambles. Jewish people everywhere desired to see the City of God once again safe, secure, and functional. Enter Nehemiah, who heard about the brokenness of the city wall from his brothers, was deeply affected by the news, and responded to God's call to take action. His preparation was his front row seat watching King Artaxerxes lead the Persian Empire. This castrated son of a prisoner of war, who served the king as part of his secret service security detail, was suddenly called to lead a construction project to rebuild a nation. The success of his leadership was built on the five words of the leadership scale. A holy partnership was formed as he listened to the call of God, saw the situation as God saw it, learned from all he heard and observed, courageously did what was needed, and loved those he served.

Listen. Leadership begins with listening, first to the voice of God and then to people.

Serving as president of my alma mater and the college attended by all our children and their spouses was both humbling and honoring. I had walked onto the campus as a student, alumnus, parent, donor, pastor, and previous member of the governing senate. But the morning I walked on as president will forever linger in my mind. As I intentionally and slowly walked through the heart of the campus to the historic building that housed my office, I was keenly aware that this was a memorable and historic walk for me. It had snowed the night before, and the facility crew had cleared the snow, creating a clean path. I found myself thinking, *The Lord has prepared the way.* Then two more thoughts suddenly popped into my mind. First, "Whether you turn to the right or to the left, your ears will hear a voice behind you, saying, 'This is the way; walk in it.'" Later that evening I took out my concordance to check whether this was a Bible verse. Sure enough, it was: Isaiah 30:21. The second thought I recognized as a Bible verse too—Proverbs 16:9: "In their hearts humans plan their course, but the LORD establishes their steps." Having these two verses randomly impressed upon my mind affirmed God's call on my life to serve in the presidential role. These two verses became my guide and foundation for the entire time I served as president. As someone once told me, "Sometimes I just look up, smile, and say, 'I know that was you. Thank you.'"

A few weeks later, at the first board meeting, I handed out cards and asked each person to write down three things that he or she wanted to see happen at the college in the next six months. Once I had tabulated the answers, I had my marching orders for the first

CHAPTER ONE

year. Also, within the first six months, I met individually or in small groups with all the employees, asking about the activities they were engaged in and their hopes, dreams, and concerns for the college. Hearing their stories and hearts' desires provided information that shaped my initial plan of action as president.

When attempting to solve problems, set goals, launch new programs, or prepare for strategic planning, listening to the people to hear their concerns, vision, and passions is important. But more important than listening to the people is listening to the voice of God. God's call to leadership and guidance along the way is one of the foundational tones to God-honoring, kingdom-seeking, biblically rooted leadership.

See. Carefully observe the various aspects of the situation and attempt to see the situation the way God sees it.

Observing the who, what, when, where, and why of a situation provides the leader with a healthy view of the perceived reality. However, as a God-honoring, kingdom-seeking, biblically rooted leader, seeing the situation as God sees it is most important. Asking, "How does God see this?" aligns the leader, helping him or her tune his or her instruments of leadership with the sound of the One who called.

While serving as a seminary dean, I was invited with a group of doctoral students to Len Sweet's home on beautiful Orcas Island. Just outside the door of his scriptorium, or what some would call a "writer's man cave," was a brown, thirty-foot-high tree trunk. It had no branches or leaves and appeared to be dead. Yet for some reason, the deck had been built around this old, dead tree trunk. "Why do you keep that old dead tree in the middle of your deck?" I asked Len. In typical Len-esque fashion, he responded, "That tree is not dead. It has more life in it than the green one behind it." Not wanting to critique the master in public, I just smiled and nodded, to which he said, "Go up to the tree and tap on it." I did. Instantly the tree was alive with movement and noise, bugs crawling all over the place. Life was evident in a new way. My eyes had deceived me. My ears did not. Often, after all our human observations, seeing a situation the way God might see it opens our leadership activity to playing a new, life-giving song. Seeing the situation as God sees it provides purpose, vision, and direction, often resulting in a third way.

Learn. Once you have heard guidance from the Lord, listened to others, observed the situation from all angles, and attempted to see it as God does, you create a new composition in your mind. This will become the music that those involved will play.

Reflecting, processing, and interpreting the sounds and sights of the situation and the people is then written as the musical score for all to learn, play, and enjoy. Asking good questions leads to clarity and sets the stage for acting. The questions usually asked are: "What have you learned?" "What does this mean?" "What actions should I take?" However, I have found three potent questions that, when collectively answered, provide clarity to most strategic decisions and action plans:

- What do you want to preserve?
- What do you want to avoid?
- What do you want to achieve?

These three questions become the key in which the music is written. Discussing and answering these questions identify desired outcomes and bring the group together as they work toward the common good. They help process the situation both cognitively and emotively.

As a leadership mentor, I always begin with these three questions. From them we establish the goals, strategies, and outcomes of our time together. It helps me identify the music those leaders desire to play, the voice and tone of their leadership, and the concerto they desire to compose.

Do. Listening, seeing, and learning have helped you evaluate the past and focus on the future. They helped you create the song you are called to direct. All that is left is to play the music. Nike® has it right: their slogan is "Just Do It." You have heard the people's concerns, received your marching orders from the Lord, observed the multitude of details, grasped how God sees the situation, and tuned the instruments to the Master Tuner. Now you need the courage to "just do it."

The actions taken may or may not be popular. The truth is, if you want to make everyone happy, sell ice cream. If you want to participate in what God is doing in the world, then respond to the call by taking action to fill God's world with his music. Of the hundreds of quotes about taking action, this one by President Theodore Roosevelt, from his famous 1910 speech "Citizenship in a Republic," says it best:

> It is not the critic who counts: not the man who points out how the strong man stumbles or where the doer of deeds could have done better. The credit belongs to the man who is actually in the arena, whose face is marred by dust and sweat and blood, who strives valiantly, who errs and comes up short again and again, because there is no effort without error or shortcoming, but who knows the great enthusiasms, the great devotions, who spends himself in a worthy cause; who, at the best, knows, in the end, the triumph of high achievement, and who, at the worst, if he fails, at least he fails while daring greatly, so that his place shall never be with those cold and timid souls who knew neither victory nor defeat.[11]

Playing the music is what you were called to do. The people never hear the song unless musicians bring the notes on the page to life.

Love. We can hear God's voice. We can see the world as God sees it. We can learn all that is needed to know. We can even have the courage to do the task. But if we do not have love, we are "a resounding gong or a clanging cymbal" (1 Corinthians 13:1). We can accomplish great things, practice outstanding faith, but if we do not have love, we "gain nothing" (13:3). The greatest expression of God's symphony is love.

At his retirement ceremony in 2003, as the Army chief of staff under President George W. Bush, General Eric Shinseki made this statement:

You must love those you lead before you can be an effective leader. You can certainly command without that sense of commitment, but you cannot lead without it. And without leadership, command is a hollow experience, a vacuum often filled with mistrust and arrogance.[12]

The military is not known for love. Yet this highly decorated four-star general with three Bronze Star Medals for valor and two Purple Hearts concluded when considering a lifetime of service that what was central in providing effective leadership was love. His words echo the words of 1 Corinthians 13.

Listen. See. Learn. Do. Love. Five words, like the chromatic scale in music, are the leadership notes upon which all God-honoring, kingdom-seeking, biblically rooted leadership activity is built. The sound of leadership repeatedly plays these tones, creating a song for all to enjoy.

> **KINGDOM TAKEAWAY**
> What words describe the framework of your leadership? In your own life and leadership, what do you want to preserve? What do you want to avoid? What do you want to achieve?

CHAPTER ONE

THE VOICE

Psalm 29:3–9

1 Kings 19:11–13

The voice of the Lord is over the waters;
the God of glory thunders,
the Lord thunders over the mighty waters.

The voice of the Lord is powerful;
the voice of the Lord is majestic.

The voice of the Lord breaks the cedars;
the Lord breaks in pieces the cedars of Lebanon.
He makes Lebanon leap like a calf,
Sirion like a young wild ox.

The voice of the Lord strikes
with flashes of lightning.

The voice of the Lord shakes the desert;
the LORD shakes the Desert of Kadesh.

The voice of the Lord twists the oaks
and strips the forests bare.

And in his temple all cry, "Glory!"

The Lord said, "Go out and stand on the mountain in the presence of the Lord, for the Lord is about to pass by."

Then a great and powerful wind tore the mountains apart and shattered the rocks before the Lord, but the Lord was not in the wind. After the wind there was an earthquake, but the Lord was not in the earthquake. After the earthquake came a fire, but the Lord was not in the fire. And after the fire came a gentle whisper. When Elijah heard it, he pulled his cloak over his face and went out and stood at the mouth of the cave.

Then a voice said to him, "What are you doing here, Elijah?"

The voice of the Lord is . . .

- powerful
- arresting
- invading
- noticeable
- attention-grabbing
- all-consuming
- soft
- tender
- gentle
- commanding

KINGDOM TAKEAWAY

Identify a time when you heard the Voice of God.

VOICES

CHAPTER TWO

DISCERNING THE VOICES

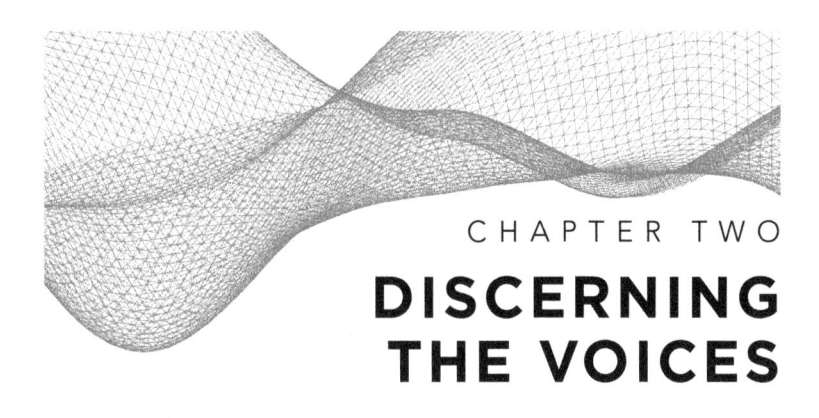

But the mob shouted louder and louder, demanding that Jesus be crucified, and their voices prevailed.
Luke 23:23 (NLT)

A man who wants to lead the orchestra must turn his back on the crowd.
Attributed to Max Lucado

People want to be heard. They desire their voices to be acknowledged and understood and their requested action to be taken. In a democratic society, freedom and expression are valued, and a minority voice expects to have an impact on the majority. Add to this our current societal climate, in which many are easily offended by the slightest phrase and immediately amplify their dissident voices on social media, creating a clash of echo chambers that require a response from their leader.

During the racial unrest and the COVID pandemic in the summer of 2020, I released a statement on behalf of the college regarding our commitment to value all people. I ran it by persons of color on campus who said it was good. I thought it was fair, transparent, and affirming. Social media erupted. Accusations flew. Demands were made. Like the howling of a tornado, some students and a few

CHAPTER TWO

alumni raised their voices in objection to the statement. Meanwhile, other constituents silently contacted me and thanked me for communicating what I had said and making the statement I did on behalf of the college. They were so thankful their college valued all people regardless of race.

Leaders make decisions. Those decisions determine the outcomes of what the leader and those he or she leads desire to accomplish or experience. Serving as a college president, I quickly learned that there were many stakeholders masquerading as self-appointed consultants, who had strong opinions about what needed to happen and what course of action I as president should take. Every decision had multiple voices attempting to influence me in the decision-making process.

Stakeholders

Board	Senior staff	Faculty	Coaches	Staff	Students
Alumni	Parents	Major donors	Donors	Perspective donors	Prospective students
Churches	Denomination	Community	City leaders	Government	Employers
Foundations	Accreditation bodies	Athletic boosters	Vendors	Partners	Banks

To understand these many voices, I mapped out all the stakeholders of the college. I identified twenty-four different major stakeholder groups, many of them having subgroups totaling an additional thirty-eight groups. Each of these groups consisted of voices who desired to have an influence on the direction and decisions of the college. I learned quickly that one of the important tasks of leadership was to discern the voices.

Early in my tenure, following an excellent board meeting, a board member approached me and kindly shared what he thought I needed to do to address the situation we had discussed. A few days later, another board member informed me what she thought was the action I needed to take regarding the same situation. The counsel of these respected board members was almost polar opposites. I realized I needed to discern these voices by something other than who was speaking.

When Jesus stood before Pilate, the religious leaders, King Herod, the crowd, Pilate's wife, and his own conscience were all speaking into the decision facing Pilate. Should he crucify Jesus or set him free? The voice of the crowd prevailed, and Pilate sentenced him to death. Pilate discerned the voices and chose to listen to the crowd.

Stakeholders continually speak. They speak with their ideas, their influence, and their money. Many of them have networks with considerable influence in society and often in the organization. The greater their involvement with the organization, the more they feel they have a right to be heard. Their motivations and demands seem justified to them as they engage with the organization. Their experiences, frame of reference, and personal values provide a conviction from which they believe their voice, whether individual or collective, is the one that needs to be heard.

Hearing the many voices of constituents and discerning which voice to honor often reveals the paradoxes of leadership. Effective leaders are required to hold in tension the multitude of competing ideas, values, and decisions. Practicing both/and rather than either/or is a leadership skill effective leaders navigate throughout their tenure.

Paradoxical decisions are constantly in play when a leader is discerning the multiple voices speaking their self-proclaimed wisdom into the leader's ears.

- Will you emphasize the importance of policy or the value of people?

- Will your budget take care of the present needs or invest in future revenues?
- Can you maintain excellence and still be affordable?
- Can you hold to the truth revealed in Scripture while demonstrating grace and compassion for all people?
- Can you communicate transparency while maintaining confidentiality?
- How do you decide when to micromanage and when to delegate and set people free?
- Can you promote creativity and innovation while maintaining the status quo?
- Do you sacrifice an individual for the good of the group or invest in developing the person's individual capacity?
- When should you be generous and when should you be frugal?
- Will you practice grace and forgiveness when costly errors are made, or will you require justice and payment for the error?
- How will you handle the voices from the margins, which are in tension with the core?
- Can you honor the past while forging a new vision for the future?
- How will you portray self-confidence while also demonstrating humility?
- When do you listen and when do you speak?

The multiple voices of the stakeholders force a leader to face these paradoxes of leadership as the leader decides which voice to honor. Often, we desire balance, but when competing voices are shouting their demands, balance is not the solution. The ability to hold the voices in tension and bring the sides together is the skill the leader needs. Learning to live with paradox is the reality of a leader.

Discerning the voices of the many stakeholders is essential for effective leadership.

For followers of Christ, living with paradoxes is nothing new. Paradoxes are central to orthodox doctrine of the Christian faith. Jesus was fully God and fully man. We are sinners and saints. We are forgiven and sinless; yet we sin constantly. Jesus is the only way; yet there are many ways to Jesus. Jesus' return is imminent; yet we wait for his return. In death we receive life. Our bodies are temporal, and our spirits are eternal. We are bound by time; yet we are eternal beings. Christianity is a paradoxical faith. So is kingdom-seeking, God-honoring, and biblically rooted leadership. Decision-making discerns the voices, intentionally choosing which voice to honor.

Holding the leadership paradoxes in tension while at the same time deciding what is a positive response requires deciding which voice is urgent and requires immediate attention, which voice is important and will need significant attention soon, which voice can wait, and which voice to ignore. Silently prioritizing the voices, the leader decides on what is the needed action to accomplish the mission and see the vision become reality.

> **KINGDOM TAKEAWAY**
> What voices are attempting to influence you to make a certain decision? What is the paradox that you need to hold in tension as you lead the group through the situation?

CHAPTER THREE

HEARING THE RIGHT VOICE

The Lord answered, "Who then is the faithful and wise manager, whom the master puts in charge of his servants to give them their food allowance at the proper time?"
Luke 12:42

You will never be criticized by someone who is doing more than you. You'll only be criticized by someone who is doing less.
Anonymous

A lie doesn't become truth, wrong doesn't become right, and evil doesn't become good just because it's accepted by a majority.
Attributed to Booker T. Washington

While serving as a college president for almost fourteen years, I made only one major decision that did not receive criticism. Most decisions, large or small, were criticized. Criticizing seemed part of the culture. Ironically, the one decision that received no criticism and had 100 percent support ended up as arguably the worst decision of my entire tenure. That decision ranks in the top three of my regrets as a college president.

Most leaders will confess that decision-making is stressful when multiple voices are clamoring for your attention and often demanding compliance with their view. Often a leader feels that he or she needs to decide which stakeholder group they want to please most. Such was the case for King Rehoboam when he succeeded his father, King Solomon, on the throne as recorded in 1 Kings 12 and 2 Chronicles 10.

Shortly after Rehoboam became king, Jeroboam and a large group of people paid a visit to the new king, requesting that he lighten the labor requirements and ease the tax burden in exchange for their pledge of loyalty, support, and service to the new king. The king asked for three days' time to consider their request, during which he first consulted his father's advisors. They encouraged the king to oblige the people. That gesture of goodwill would yield a lifetime of service from his subjects. Rehoboam then asked his inner circle, who were also his childhood friends, what they thought he should do. These young bucks, with limited leadership experience, had swallowed the power pill. They advised King Rehoboam to instead increase his demands and make the people's burden even heavier. Show them who is boss. When Jeroboam and his group returned, King Rehoboam informed them their burden would be doubled. Realizing the king had not listened to them, the people rejected Rehoboam as king, rebelled against his authority, and pledged their allegiance to Jeroboam. No one knows for sure what was going through Rehoboam's mind, but the inexperienced voices of his peers held sway over the wise voices of the elders who had served his father. Rehoboam listened to the wrong voices. The price for discerning the wrong voices and listening to the wrong advisors was losing five-sixth of his kingdom.

Every person who occupies a C-suite is as effective as the senior leadership personnel around him or her. The demands of the role require a loyal, competent, wise, and transparent staff. As the saying goes, a leader is only as good as the people around him or her. Leaders' voices often communicate the hopes and dreams of the people whom they are called to serve. Their ears hear the various stakeholders' thoughts and desires. Strategies are implemented, problems are solved, and challenges are addressed by the staff. Their voices are invaluable when attempting to discern which voices to honor.

When I first began serving in the role of a college president, I asked each of my direct reports four questions:

1. What are the basic responsibilities of your role?
2. What do you need from me to be successful?
3. What is something you think I need to know about the college?
4. What will make me a successful president?

Hearing their voices helped me understand how we could work together to fulfill our common mission as a college. Their voices shaped my understanding of the role. In subsequent years, I would ask additional questions that would continually shape my leadership service:

1. Where have I helped you succeed in your role and responsibility?
2. Where have I been a hindrance to you in carrying out your responsibility?
3. List one thing that I should keep doing as president.
4. List one thing that you would like me to do differently.

These voices were important to me as I attempted to wisely carry out my responsibilities as president. Doing the right thing at the right time in the right way and for the right reason was a song everyone loved hearing.

The importance of the people around the leader and making sure all voices are heard can best be illustrated when facing a crisis. Early in my tenure as president, one of our students was murdered by a student from a neighboring college. The voices were numerous telling us how we should respond. The parents and family of the deceased were heartbroken and wanted answers to their questions and justice for the accused. The press was constantly looking for a sensational story, inciting emotional responses with their accusatory questions. Our lawyer was cautioning us to limit our exposure. Medical professionals gave advice attempting to save the student's life. Law enforcement was investigating the crime. The neighboring college was concerned about its image. We were attempting to control the publicity frenzy on campus. Our students were grieving the loss of a friend and teammate. Everyone had a valid voice and needed to be heard. Having a strong team in place to deal with the various aspects of the crisis and make sure I heard all the voices was invaluable. Allowing people to speak and validating their voices by listening to them helped us navigate a very difficult situation. I was surprised that simply spending time with those involved, asking clarifying questions, and presenting the facts as they came to light, provided the validation each voice desired.

In most cases, senior leadership is privy to more information than is appropriate for the public to know. Although transparency is a good thing in effective leadership, often some information is best not made public due to privacy issues, legal issues, or the risk of embarrassment for some of the stakeholders.

When engaging in conversation regarding strategic initiatives with the potential to alter an organization's culture, hearing the people's voices clarifies and assists in preparing for desired change. Ideas regarding vision and values are communicated. Skills required to implement change will surface. Incentives and resources needed are brought to your attention. All this information will reduce confusion, anxiety, and frustration; lessen mission drift; and speed up the change process. Quite possibly, an action plan will come into view as you assimilate all the voices into one harmonious song. You still need to make decisions. However, you are not making them blindly. The voices have informed your thinking, creating the possibility of loyalty and support by the people most affected by the desired change.

As with all change, when voices offer differing perspectives, it is good to remember three things:

- The majority voice is not always the right voice.
- The loud voice is not always the right voice.
- The passionate voice is not always the right voice.

Discerning the voices is not as simple as taking a vote. In a democratic society, the majority gets their way. Some of your stakeholder groups may assume that if most of the group wants the decision to go a certain way, then you should simply allow the majority to rule. People forget that most organizations are not democracies. As a friend of mine would often say, "This is not a democracy. It is a theocracy, and I am Theo." As the plaque on President Harry Truman's desk stated for all to see, "The buck stops here."[13]

At times, stakeholder groups might amplify their voices by using social media, organizational publications, or community forums, attempting to present their case as a very strong and heavily supported idea. At these times during my tenure, there was lots of activity. Treatises were written and posted in public places, often using the Scriptures to bolster their case. Letters were written to the board and editorials submitted to the local paper. I would listen and work hard to practice the golden rule of "Do to others as you would have them do to you" (Matthew 7:12). I consistently sought to meet face-to-face with the leader of the respective group so I could fully understand their concern. However, in the end, the volume of their collective voice was not what influenced my decision.

I found it interesting when a stakeholder group would inform me how passionate they were about the point they were making, as if intensity and determination were the reasons I should listen to their voice. But if someone is sincere but they are wrong, then they are sincerely wrong.

The attempted influence of the majority voice, the loudest voice, or the most passionate voice most often surfaces when strategic decisions are discussed, personnel are being hired, or policy decisions regarding political ideologies enter the conversation. The natural response is to listen to the majority or the loud and passionate voices. But these are not always the right voice. A different decision-making mechanism is required.

> **KINGDOM TAKEAWAY**
>
> When many voices are clamoring for your attention, how do you determine which voice to listen to? What questions do you ask to demonstrate you are genuinely seeking to hear and understand their concerns?

CHAPTER FOUR

DECIDING ON WHICH VOICE

> *Whether you turn to the right or to the left, your ears will hear a voice behind you, saying, "This is the way; walk in it."*
> **Isaiah 30:21**

> *I am not a product of my circumstances.
> I am a product of my decisions.*
> **Stephen R. Covey,** *The Wisdom and Teachings of Stephen R. Covey*

The responsibility to decide whose voice to honor rests with the person in charge. The acoustical art of determining the right voice is a skill both innate and learned. Deciding on which voice to listen to is like identifying the key of a musical composition, hearing the pitch, and then singing it a cappella. When music is amplified, frequencies are isolated and filters are applied to enhance the sound the producer desires. Deciding which voice to listen to requires the ability to distinguish the musical key and apply the needed filters to enhance the sound for those hearing the rendition.

The pitch, key, and filters together help the leader choose to do the right thing at the right time in the right way for the right reason. Although the decision can at times seem political in nature, it must demonstrate integrity and relevance. When deciding whose voice to listen to, there are five filters through which the multiple voices must pass: mission, vision, values, resources, and the Voice of One.

After serving eight years in the role of president, I was convinced we needed a new, sustainable business model. For three years we worked on developing a new model. Many stakeholder groups spoke into the value proposition, the margin formula, the key processes and resources, and the metrics that would be used to monitor and evaluate.[14] Often the discussion was with sincere convictions and divergent views. As I listened to the many voices, the filters through which I evaluated all the commentary was extremely helpful. The decisions made all passed through the five filters. In the end we had a new business model that was sustainable, along with an opportunity to rebrand the organization, preparing it for a preferred future.

The filter of mission. Every decision, large or small, should help fulfill the mission of the organization. Preserving why you exist, avoiding mission drift, and achieving the desired mission effect are the outcomes of the mission filter. The voices that help you accomplish what you want to preserve, avoid, and achieve are the voices you need to follow. This filter's primary purpose is keeping the entire organization aligned with the mission and playing in the same key. Various stakeholder groups often have shadow missions that can introduce minor keys to a composition written in a major key. Keeping the main thing the main thing is the number one responsibility of leadership.

The filter of vision. What you want the organization to become as you live out your mission greatly influences deciding whose voice to honor. Decisions you make should turn opportunities into realities. Voices that move your organization toward fulfilling the preferred future and desired reality should be honored. Often the voices have misconceptions about vision. Naturally we think of vision as seeing what can happen in the future. However, our eyes are prone to deceive us and trick us into seeing something different from reality. All of us have looked at pictures in which two different images can

CHAPTER FOUR

be seen depending on where you look. Vision is the foresight of the desired outcome of a mission accomplished. Deciding whose voice to honor should advance the preferred future of the organization.

The filter of values. Significant to any organization are the shared values of the group. What are the deepest held convictions that form the foundation of who you are? Voices that contradict your values need to be discarded. Voices that affirm and honor your values should be adhered to. Often what is stated as the shared values are not what is most important to the group. Values are deeply held convictions that if taken away, would cause internal hurt leading to anger. If you want to know the real values, look at how money is spent, which actions are rewarded, and how time and energy are allocated. Then ask the big question that reveals the real values: What, if taken away, would cause great anger?

The filter of resources. You can have an honorable mission, a clear vision, and solid values. But if your organization has no money to pay for it, then the decision on what to do is quite simple. As someone once said, "The only thing that matters is the mission and the money to pay for it." When multiple voices are telling you what to do, in the end, the one having the resources to implement is the one you listen to. All presidents of nonprofit organizations are bi-vocational fundraisers. Kingdom-seeking, God-honoring, biblically rooted organizations are engaged in a holy partnership with the God who moves people's hearts to contribute to your mission and vision. You are responsible to practice good stewardship, make wise choices, and clearly communicate the vision and mission. But it is the God who has called you who moves the hearts of the people to provide the resources for you to accomplish the mission. Just as God has placed in you a desire to accomplish a mission, so God has placed in the hearts of others a desire to contribute to the mission.

The Voice of One. Mission, vision, and values for kingdom-seeking, God-honoring, biblically rooted leadership involves clarifying the mission, identifying a preferred future that comes from hearing the Voice of One and having the courage to take the action the Voice is calling you to take. Providing it is not misused or abused, the Voice of One filter supersedes all others.

When Jesus walked this earth, his decision mechanism was very simple: he only did what he saw his heavenly Father do (John 5:19). Leaders who desire to honor God with the stewardship of their life and leadership need to listen to Jesus' voice, see the situation as he sees it, learn from him, have the courage to do what he asks, and above all, walk in love.

A biblical example of deciding whose voice to listen to while also honoring the Voice of One is found in Acts 15, where the early church met in Jerusalem to make a significant decision about how the followers of Jesus would move forward regarding religious rituals and commitments.

Because of the missionary activity of Paul and Barnabas, the young church in Acts was faced with non-Jewish people becoming part of "the Way." Which Jewish rituals would be required for new believers from non-Jewish backgrounds to experience salvation? The Jewish believers with a Pharisee background conflicted with the voices of those who were evangelizing the non-Jewish world. All sides gathered in Jerusalem to discuss the matter. The leadership paradox was the classic core/margins paradox. The final decision took into consideration the mission, vision, and values of the movement. Proclaiming the good news to everyone regardless of their ethnic background and affirming the freedom Christ brings to those who follow him was honored. The letter communicating the decision clearly affirmed the group was listening to the Voice of One: "It seemed good to the Holy Spirit and to us . . ." (Acts 15:28). All voices had spoken, and the filters amplified the decision to the churches in the region. The mission, vision, and values of proclaiming the gospel to everyone (the mission) with groups of believers growing throughout the Roman Empire (the vision) committed to wholesome living (the values) became the filtersthrough which the young church decided on whose voice to honor, creating a harmonious chorus.

Significant to the decision were the sound elements that brought about the agreement. "The whole assembly became *silent* as they *listened* to Paul and Barnabas *telling* about the miraculous signs and wonders God had done among the Gentiles though them" (Acts 15:12, emphasis added). Hearing the stories gave way to the written law of Moses.

When deciding on whose voice to listen to, it is essential to understand the mission of God in the world. Scripture records one story that answers the question, What is God doing in the world? That story is recorded in Exodus 5:22–6:8.

Moses had answered the call to lead God's people out of slavery in Egypt. Reluctantly he went to Pharaoh, asking him to let the people go. Pharaoh's response was to heartlessly increase their workload. The people were furious and blamed Moses for their new misery. Moses was hot. He had done what God called him to do; yet his obedience had resulted in all the people being mad at him. For the second time in his life, his own people were against him. So, Moses had a heart-to-heart, highly emotive talk with the Lord.[15] "Why . . . ? You said . . . I did . . . You have not kept your word . . . God, what are you doing?"

God replied, "Watch me . . . I am the LORD . . . Trust me . . . I will deliver the people . . . I will take them as my own . . . They will know that I am the LORD . . . I will bring them to a land . . . ." And that is what happened. The book of Exodus along with Leviticus, Numbers, and Deuteronomy, chronicle the story of God honoring the action plans announced to Moses. The action plan answered Moses's question.

The story does not end there. The four pillars of God's action plan become themes throughout the Scriptures of what God is up to in the world. In Ezekiel 34, when the word of the Lord came to Ezekiel about the shepherds of the people, these four pillars were again highlighted. "I will rescue my flock . . . I will gather them . . . I will bring them into their own land . . . They will know I am the LORD."

Hundreds of years later, God's Son appeared on the earth. The words of Jesus, as recorded in the Gospels, reiterate God's activity on the earth. Jesus himself said, "I have come to seek and save that which was lost" (Luke 19:10 paraphrased); "I will build my church" (Matthew 16:18); "Anyone who has seen me has seen the father" (John 14:9); "I have come that they might have life . . . to the full" (John 10:10). These words identify Jesus' work on earth fulfilling the mission of God.

The early church, as recorded in Acts, continued implementing the action plans of God, bringing salvation to all, enjoying fellowship, connecting with the Lord, and providing a better life. And it does not stop there. Revelation 21:1–4 identifies how God's action plans play out in the hereafter:

> Then I saw "a new heaven and a new earth," for the first heaven and the first earth had passed away, and there was no longer any sea. I saw the Holy City, the new Jerusalem, coming down out of heaven from God, prepared as a bride beautifully dressed for her husband. And I heard a loud voice from the throne saying, "Look! God's dwelling place is now among the people, and he will dwell with them. They will be his people, and God himself will be with them and be their God. 'He will wipe every tear from their eyes. There will be no more death' or mourning or crying or pain, for the old order of things has passed away."

What is God up to in the world? He is bringing deliverance. He is forming community. He is helping us to know him. He is giving us a quality life. Together, this is the fourfold purpose of God. God's response to Moses resulted in themes throughout the Scriptures revealing his purpose on earth.[16] This is what God has, is, and will do. His purpose is (1) to bring deliverance, (2) to form community, (3) to enable us to know him, and (4) to provide a good life for his people. When deciding on whose voice to listen to, voices that equip and inspire you to participate with God in fulfilling his mission in the world are voices worthy of your honor and respect. Your decision will be a small part of God's activity in the world.

CHAPTER FOUR

> **KINGDOM TAKEAWAY**
> When forced to make difficult decisions, what filters do you apply to the decision-making process? How are your decisions participating in the mission of God in the world?

CHAPTER FIVE

LISTENING TO THE VOICE OF ONE

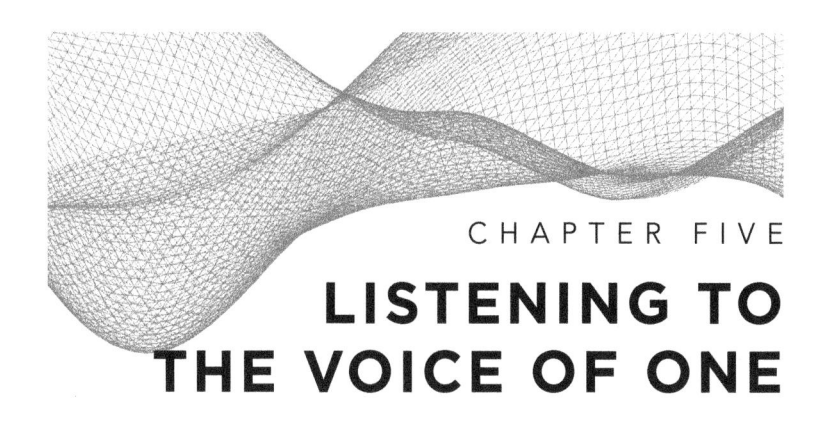

"The Son can do nothing by himself. He does only what he sees the Father doing. Whatever the Father does, the Son also does."
John 5:19 (NLT)

When I walk with God, He does the talking. He also determines the pace of the walking as well as the route!
Attributed to Stephan Joubert

Let me ask you some questions.

- Do you believe God is alive and active in the world today?
- Do you believe that God is still speaking?
- Do you believe that God has your best interest in mind?
- Do you believe that God wants the group you lead to thrive?

If you answered yes to these questions, then listening to the Voice of One is not a wise choice but also a reasonable, relevant, and required choice for effective kingdom-seeking, God-honoring, biblically rooted leadership.

CHAPTER FIVE

Our model for listening to the Voice of One is Jesus. He lived a God-arranged life continually listening to the voice of his Father instructing him on actions he took.

In John 5, Jesus entered what might be called a "divine healing hospital" of that day. Many disabled people in need of healing were lying around the pool. Jesus singled out one who had been paralyzed for thirty-eight years and said, "Get up! Pick up your mat and walk" (John 5:8). The man stood to his feet, bent over, picked up his mat, and walked.

The religious leaders questioned Jesus' activity because he had healed on the Sabbath. My question would be, Why did he only heal one? Jesus answered both questions:

> My Father is always at his work to this very day, and I too am working. . . . The Son can do nothing by himself; he can do only what he sees his Father doing, because whatever the Father does the Son also does (John 5:17, 19).

Jesus followed this pattern.

In John 4, when Jesus decided to leave Judea and go to Galilee, instead of crossing the Jordan River and traveling on the eastern side of the river, avoiding the shorter route through Samaria so as not to come in contact with a marginalized group, he chose to walk through Samaria. His journey led him to an exchange with a nameless woman at a well, drawing water at an unusual time of day, resulting in many Samaritans believing in him. John simply says, "Now he *had* to go through Samaria" (v. 4, emphasis added). He *had* to? It was as if Jesus heard the Father saying, "I have this woman who is ready to receive our good news. She will be at a well near Sychar. I want you to travel through Samaria and talk with her." So, Jesus deliberately walked through Samaria.

When news that Lazarus was sick reached Jesus, he waited two days before telling his disciples, "Let us go back to Judea" (John 11:7). Again, it was as if his Father were saying, "Wait . . . Wait . . . Wait . . . Now go." Why the wait? Evidently the Father wanted to demonstrate his power through the raising of Lazarus from the dead. Jesus was simply doing the work his Father was doing.

Another example is when Jesus was walking between Jericho and Jerusalem. Crowds of people were along the road. A short man who was despised by everyone was hiding in a tree just to get a glimpse of Jesus passing by. Except Jesus did not pass by. He stopped, looked up into the tree, asked the man to come down, and invited himself to the man's home. The man experienced forgiveness and made a gigantic expression of repentance (Luke 19:1–10). Again, it is as if Jesus were walking along the road and the Father whispered into his ear, "Stop and talk to that short man whom everyone hates. He is in a tree. He is ready for our message." Jesus was so in tune with the Father that as he moved through life, he heard the voice of his Father calling him to engage with selected people. He lived from a divine center, participating with the Father in his mission in his world. Each supernatural encounter Jesus had with people revealed the presence and activity of God in the world.

During the years I served as pastor, I would attempt regularly to get away for a time of solitude and silence. Over time I discovered that sometimes God would speak, sometimes God would be silent, and sometimes, he would just hold me. One of the times I remember very well, he spoke. I had completed all the coursework for my doctoral degree. I had completed my research and written about 75 percent of my dissertation. But rather than complete it, I began to implement what I had learned. I saw no need to finish writing just to receive a paper with my name and degree on it. I had entered the program to learn about leadership so I could be a better pastor. That objective was completed. I saw no need to finish. While I was seated in a hammock at the Quiet House at Laity Lodge in west Texas, meditating, praying, and journaling, a strong impression out of nowhere lodged in my mind that I could not shake. It was as if the Lord had said to me, "*Go home and finish writing your dissertation for the work I have for you.*" Not having a clue what this meant, I went home and followed that guidance, which I understood as having come from the Voice of One. I contacted Fuller Seminary and discovered that I had just more three months to complete the work without having to start over on the dissertation. I quickly finished writing, sent the document snail mail, and within the month received a copy back, instructing me what I needed to change. I made the changes just in time to meet the deadline and walk across the stage to receive my diploma. One year later I was invited to serve as dean of the seminary at George Fox University. Without a doctoral degree, this invitation would never have come. Six years later, my alma mater called, asking to talk with me about becoming their president. The doctoral degree was an important part of my résumé.

Listening to the Voice of One leads to living a God-arranged life in which the variation of the tones of the leadership scale (listen, see, learn, do, and love) become a concert of service and praise. Mission, vision, values, and resources are important when discerning the multiple and varied voices of the stakeholders. But the Voice of One trumps all other voices. His voice calls, equips, and inspires us to participate with him in his activity in the world.

Learning to hear the Voice of One can only happen as we get to know the One speaking. When Jesus described himself as the good shepherd, he said, "The one who enters by the gate is the shepherd of the sheep. The gatekeeper opens the gate for him, and the sheep listen to his voice. He calls his own sheep by name and leads them out. When he has brought out all his own, he goes on ahead of them, and his sheep follow him because they know his voice. But they will never follow a stranger; in fact, they will run away from him because they do not recognize a stranger's voice" (John 10:2–5).

Like answering the phone and recognizing the voice of a familiar caller, so continually walking with God, engaging in conversation with him, and heeding his directions enables us to identify his voice when he speaks.

The resurrection story as told in John demonstrates the power of recognizing and *hearing* the Voice of One. In John 20, the gospel writer uses four different Greek words to describe what people *saw* that morning. In verse 1, Mary was visually aware (*blepo*) that the stone had been moved. In verses 12 and 14, she looked attentively (*theoreo*) at the angels and at Jesus. When John arrived, he examined (*eidon*) the empty tomb. And in verse 18, Mary experienced (*horao*) Jesus. But it was his voice that caused Mary to recognize him.[17] When Jesus said her name, "Mary," her eyes stopped tricking her (she had at first thought he was the gardener). She recognized his voice. When our ears hear the Voice of One, we can distinguish and discern what we are called to do.

Emphasizing the Voice of One can be dangerous. Many of us have experienced the shadow side of a leader who boldly proclaims, "God told me to _____." You fill in the blank. Suggesting we learn to listen to the Voice of One can cause some consternation. However, I firmly believe that kingdom-seeking, God-honoring, biblically rooted leadership needs to learn how to hear God's voice. Leaders must lead from a divine center with a heart in tune with the heart of God, forming a holy partnership that results in fulfilling the purposes of God on earth.

> **KINGDOM TAKEAWAY**
>
> Think of a time you were convinced the Voice of One had spoken and you listened to it. In your mind, relive that situation. How did the Voice of One equip and inspire you to listen?

MUSIC

INTERLUDE
MUSIC AND LEADERSHIP

"Music is generally defined as the art of arranging sound to create some combination of form, harmony, melody, rhythm or otherwise expressive content. Exact definitions of music vary considerably around the world, though it is an aspect of all human societies, a cultural universal. While scholars agree that music is defined by a few specific elements, there is no consensus on their precise definitions."[18]

Leadership, like music, has no exact definition and varies from society to society. Each scholar, author, or popular speaker communicates a unique understanding and definition of leadership. Most people would define leadership as the act of influencing a group of people toward a preferred future. It involves an encounter between two or more persons and has to do with moving into the future. As John Maxwell, stated, "He that thinketh he leadeth, and hath no one following, is only taking a walk."[19] The root of the word *lead* comes from the Old English, meaning "to go."[20] Like music, the combined elements of leadership create an inspiring expression for those experiencing the leadership encounter.

Over one hundred times the Scriptures record people singing and making music to the Lord, offering him praise. Ironically, we have only one record of Jesus singing or engaging in music. After Jesus ate his final Passover meal with his disciples "they sang a hymn" (Mark 14:26 NLT). I am not sure why Jesus did not engage more with music, except that it gives hope to those who cannot carry a tune. Rarely is the early church encouraged to sing songs. In Ephesians we are commanded to "sing and make music from your heart to the Lord" (5:19). However, music does not seem to be central to the early church. Evidently an artist did not write any of the four Gospels or the letters to the churches. Still, the book of Revelation tells us that music is a heavenly activity, and we know that fifty-five Hebrew psalms were written for a "director of music." (See, for example, the openings of Psalms 4–6.)

Music and leadership are creative, life shaping, inspiring, and relevant expressions of the One who influences the world.

> **KINGDOM TAKEAWAY**
> What song best personifies your personal leadership soundtrack?

CHAPTER SIX
ENROLLING IN GOD'S SCHOOL OF MUSIC

For we are God's masterpiece. He has created us anew in Christ Jesus, so we can do the good things he planned for us long ago.
Ephesians 2:10 (NLT)

. . . speaking to one another with psalms, hymns, and songs from the Spirit. Sing and make music from your heart to the Lord.
Ephesians 5:19

Leadership is authentic self-expression that creates value.
Kevin Cashman, *Leadership from the Inside Out*

I was forced to go to high school. I begged my parents not to make me go. I wanted to farm and thought school was a waste of energy. My dad had six weeks of high school and was a successful farmer. Why did I need to attend high school?

I was enticed to go to college. My parents asked me to go just one year. So, I obliged them. I enjoyed the newfound freedom, recognized vocational opportunities in addition to farming, got married between my sophomore and junior years, and realized finishing college was a good thing.

CHAPTER SIX

I recognized the need to go to seminary when I sensed God's call on my life to pursue vocational ministry. I went and enjoyed the challenge of study and the joy of learning.

I realized the world was changing and I wanted to learn more about ministry in a changing world. So, while pastoring, I pursued a doctorate. The topic of leadership captured my imagination, and I enjoyed exploring the depths of the topic.

Here is the kicker. For twenty years I led educational institutions, with the final chapter of my vocational life leading a Christian college for fourteen of those years. What a sense of humor God has. When I reflect on my learning journey, I am still in awe at the path the Lord himself designed and prepared for me to travel. A South Dakota farm boy who hates school, serving Christ by leading an academic institution. That is so God.

God is in the business of developing people to provide leadership service fulfilling his mission in the world. From the beginning of time, he has called individuals, inspired and equipped them for service, and sent them into his world, making it more as he intended it to be. He has an affinity for selecting the least, the smallest, and the unlikeliest characters, inspiring them with a mission and vision beyond their ability, assigning them a task beyond their capacity, and along the way shaping and molding them to be the influencer he wants them to be. Like a composer, he arranges the notes of their lives, creating a melody complete with harmonic sounds that become a masterpiece for all to enjoy.

Scripture is full of individuals whom God called. He communicated a desired outcome beyond their capacity to even imagine, asked for total buy-in, and then equipped and inspired them to begin seeing his desire become a reality. Whenever God calls someone to a task, it is always larger than any one person can accomplish. His request for you to serve is never like someone asking you to help with the local PTO: "It won't take much of your time, and it is not hard work." No, God's call always requires complete commitment and skills beyond one's ability. His requests are beyond our imagination. Often, we will not see the final result in our lifetimes. A few examples:

- Abram: "Leave . . . go . . . I will make you into a great nation" (Genesis 12:1–2). Hundreds of years later, a nation was born.

- Joseph: There is no recorded communication from God but a litany of abuse, hurt, and pain. Years later Joseph stated, "God intended it for good to accomplish what is now being done, the saving of many lives" (Genesis 50:20).

- Moses: "I hear the cry of my people . . . Go lead them out . . . bring them into a good and spacious land." Generations later it happened.

- Joshua: "Go cross the Jordan . . . every place you walk will be yours." At the end of his life, there were still "very large areas of land to be taken over" (Joshua 1 and 13).

- David: "I will establish a house for you, a kingdom and throne that will endure forever." A century later Jesus arrived on the earth to establish his kingdom forever (2 Samuel 7; Luke 1).

- Peter: "On this rock I will build my church" (Matthew 16:18). Millennia later, the church is still being built (see 1 Corinthians 3).

- Twelve disciples: "Go and make disciples of all nations" (Matthew 28:19). The command is still being fulfilled today.

- Saul and Barnabas: "Set them apart for the work I have for them . . . Preach Jesus among the Gentiles." That task is still happening today (Acts 13).

- John: "Show . . . what must soon take place." We are still waiting for the return of Jesus (Revelation 1:1).

CHAPTER SIX

Even the "Faith Hall of Fame," recorded in Hebrews 11, ends with the words, "These were all commended for their faith, yet none of them received what had been promised" (v. 39).

The mission of God in the world is carried out by individuals who allow the Lord to shape their lives, preparing them for meaningful leadership service. Like the sound of a beautiful symphony, their lives inspire those around them, bringing hope, peace, and fulfillment.

Everyone is called to serve. Some are chosen to lead. God takes great delight in creating individual masterpieces that sing his songs and play his music to the world. His curriculum incorporates all the different musical sounds to produce a masterpiece enjoyed by all who hear it. Over a lifetime, each of us is written into a harmonious symphony pleasing to the ear. Every aspect of our life is incorporated into the composition. Our *sovereign foundations*, like our families of origin, growing-up environments, and historical events, are the basis of the score. The *inner-life growth* of knowing God, responding in obedience to him, and listening to him, form a continuous, repetitive theme in the composition. *Maturing in ministry* by discovering one's giftedness, cultivating meaningful relationships, and assuming roles of service form the overarching theme of the music. *Life maturation*, including every broken world and personal best experience, individuals who have influenced you, and life experiences that have brought satisfaction and fruitfulness, are woven into the song. The music crescendos to a *convergence*, where all the experiences and influences of one's life come together as a grand finale. Then suddenly the music shifts; the sounds soften and gently reward a life of Christian service as a kind of *afterglow*, in which one responds to requests of those seeking to hear the wisdom gained over the years. That influence happens exclusively through relationships. The composition finishes well with a reverent "Amen."[21]

As individuals chosen to lead God's people in fulfilling his purposes on earth, we are enrolled in a school in which each person is a masterpiece created by the good hand of the Master Musician and

Conductor, the Originator of all music. Every aspect of our lives has purpose and meaning in the school of God.

In the summer of 2007, I received a phone call that resulted in my accepting an invitation to become the president of my alma mater. The thought of serving in a presidential role had never crossed my mind. As I hung up the phone, my face turned ashen, my hands began to shake, and my knuckles turned white. I escaped out the back door of my office into the parking lot to get some air. A few months later, the board of directors issued a formal invitation for me to assume the role. My wife, Peg, and I immediately left for the Oregon coast to spend the weekend at our favorite getaway place. During the weekend, we prayed, tried to imagine what the role would entail, and reviewed our entire lives of ministry and leadership service. As we processed the invitation and reflected on twenty-five years of pastoral ministry and six years of serving as dean of a seminary, we suddenly realized all along that we had been prepared for such a time as this. Experience after experience and what we had learned along the way seemed to point to preparation for assuming the presidential role. My undergraduate business degree, graduate theological training, and doctoral work in leadership would be put to good use. Various leadership challenges we had overcome, our personal bests, and our broken world experiences all had a tone that seemed to fit the key of our next leadership service assignment. My pastoral heart, weekly public speaking, and working with teams seemed like rehearsals for what felt to us like preparation for a concert at Carnegie Hall. Our sovereign foundations, inner-life growth, and life and ministry maturation were converging in a leadership service role we had never imagined. Without our knowing it, the Lord had prepared us for this time and place.

The personal vision, mission, and image statements I had created decades earlier under the mentorship of the Lord became vital to this new experience. As a seasoned vocal coach would train a student, God's voice guided me to put into words the focus and direction of my life. A pitch pipe for my life and mission, this statement provided

CHAPTER SIX

the sound by which I lived my life and the tuning key for how my major decisions would be made. When I reviewed my mission statement "to honor and trust God with my life by being a person of influence, impacting and inspiring with relevance and integrity the lives of those who will influence others," it seemed 100 percent in tune with serving in the role of a president of a Christian college. Even my image statement (the pilot wheel of a ship) became appropriate to the responsibilities I would assume. God's call on my life was affirmed as I processed the invitation.

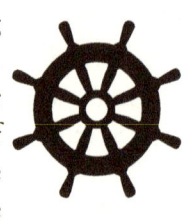

Each of us represent a masterpiece composition of the Lord. Like a songwriter, God creates a song with the experiences of our lives that fulfills his purposes. In return, our lives become a harmonious sound to him as we serve the situation he has called us to influence. Each of us is shaped by the sovereign hand of God into the leader we are today and will be in the future.

> **KINGDOM TAKEAWAY**
>
> How have the experiences of your life shaped you into the person you are today? How have these experiences prepared you for your current leadership calling?

CHAPTER SEVEN
COMPOSING YOUR SONG

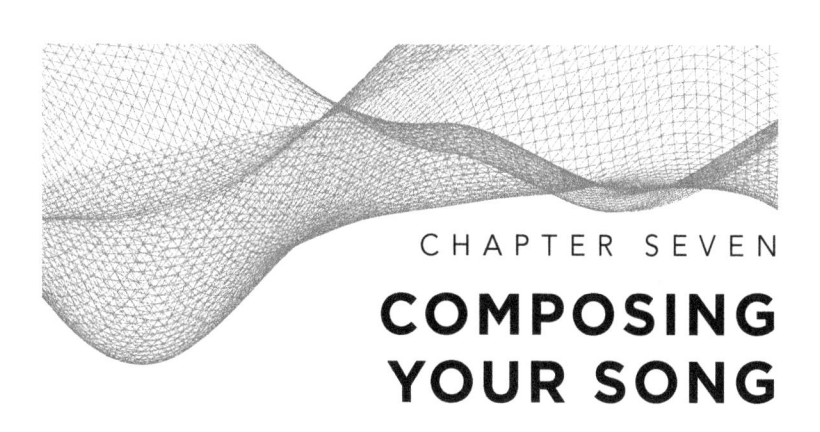

You saw me before I was born.
Every day of my life was recorded in your book.
Every moment was laid out
before a single day had passed.
Psalms 139:16 (NLT)

For God is working in you, giving you the desire and the power to
do what pleases him.
Philippians 2:13 (NLT)

Leadership is an art, a performing art. And . . . the artist's
instrument is the self. The mastery of the art of leadership comes
with the mastery of the self.
James M. Kouzes and Barry Z. Posner, *The Leadership Challenge*

Never regard something as doing you good if it makes you betray
a trust, or lose your sense of shame, or makes you show hatred,
suspicion, ill will, or hypocrisy, or a desire for things best done
behind closed doors.
Marcus Aurelius, *Meditations*

CHAPTER SEVEN

Leadership is being that results in doing. Who you are determines how you lead. How you lead flows from who you are. The song of our lives and leadership heard over the loudspeakers by those we influence comes from the composition of our sovereign foundations expressed in an array of attitudes, actions, and style. Our personhood is lived out in our persona. The song people hear is our personae, which reveals who we are.

Eighty percent of you is like the rest of humanity. We each have two arms, legs, eyes, and ears. We each have one head, nose, mouth, tongue, and a host of other organs in our bodies. All of us have emotions, personalities, likes, dislikes, and values.

Fifteen percent of us are similar yet different. The color of our eyes, the length of our arms and legs, and the color of our hair are different from one another's. We all have bodies, but in different shapes. Our individual emotional responses and personalities are different from most others'.

A remaining 5 percent of each of us is totally unique. The combination of our heritage, birth order, places we grew up, experiences we have had, and choices we have made are totally unique to each of us. God made only one of each of us. As the popular saying goes, "After God made you, he threw away the mold."

Personality, strengths, values, sovereign foundations, events, personal bests, and broken world experiences in life all have shaped us into the persons we are today. Who we are is expressed with a set of behavioral tendencies, a leadership personality, and a certain style. How a person understands mission, embraces vision, employs strategies, solves problems, sets direction, equips and inspires teams, and approaches planning are all a natural expression of who he or she is. A leader's voice, tone, and mood are an expression of his or her inner being.

The inscription "Know thyself," carved above the entrance of the ancient temple of the Greek god Apollo, is appropriate advice for every leader. Over the years I have taken a variety of assessments, helping me understand myself. They all have come back with the same basic idea, although using different words to fit their respective model. I am a visionary leader with a creative, action-oriented style that engages people, and I am principle driven. Myers–Briggs, Clifton Strengthfinders, DiSC, Culture Index, Professional DynaMetric Programs, Working Genius, StandOut, the Leadership Personality Test, EQ-i, the ECI (Emotional Competence Inventory), Enneagram, MMPI . . . all of these together provide a picture of who I am and what you can expect of me as I lead an organization.

Leading out of who we are is natural and does not require a set of goals or a personal plan. It just happens. My predecessor was an ESTJ with a master's in psychology, served in the mental health field as a CEO before becoming a college president, and was an enterprising administrator. Every administrative position had a position description. Yearly evaluations were conducted, and a meticulous strategic plan was implemented. Policies were followed, and relational health was important. My successor was an ISTP with a Ph.D. in computer science, was a tenured professor at a prestigious university before becoming president, and was a philosophic academician. An emphasis on shared governance, a rewrite of the policy manual, and a focus on traditional residential Christian liberal arts education became the strategic direction of the college. Raising the bar of academics became the college's informal strategic plan. My tenure came in between these two capable leaders. I am an ENFJ with a D.Min. in leadership and church management, served as pastor and seminary dean before becoming president, and am a trailblazing practitioner. I lived in the future, taking risks, tackling projects many thought could not happen, and delegating operations to trusted staff. I was highly concerned about our theological identity, and I focused almost exclusively on the big picture.

Each of us led the college differently. With my predecessor, the college ran smoothly, with healthy relationships. My visionary, action-oriented style was disruptive and produced many tensions yet significant accomplishments. My successor pivoted the college, desiring to consolidate operations.

My predecessor lived life gently and held a balance between people and task orientation. I lived life boldly and was people oriented. My successor lived life gently and was task oriented.

The mission stayed the same, but the vision, values, tone, and mood of the college differed significantly with each leader. The voices we listened to, how we solved problems, worked with teams, set strategic direction, and implemented initiatives all were extremely different and fit our respective identities. Each of us was true to who we were as individuals as we led the college. Each of us had experienced God working in us and were pleasing God with our leadership.

All of us are shaped by the hand of God. The sovereign foundations of our heritage, race, and family legacy coupled with broken world experiences, personal bests, painful challenges, and scars of abuse all have served to shape us for such a time as this. We are God's works of art, his masterpieces. He is shaping us into the leaders he wants us to be to fulfill his mission in the world.

When Scripture describes the leadership of King David, it states simply that he led with "integrity of heart" and "skillful hands" (Psalm 78:72). During his reign, David had spectacular accomplishments achieved with a sincere heart. Character and competency, person and persona, heart and hands/feet, each of these duets is needed to provide effective leadership. Like the treble and bass clefs, matters of the heart and the actions we employ together create a full sound. The heart gives impetus to our actions, and our actions reveal our hearts. Therefore, "above all else, guard your heart, for everything you do flows from it" (Proverbs 4:23). As educator and businessman Stephen Covey stated, "Private victories precede public victories."[22] Take care of your heart.

Given this relationship between who we are and how we lead, tending to matters of the heart is the leader's first priority. The song you are composing requires you understand yourself, cultivate good character, and identify the values that are important to you.

Back in the 1990s, when worship bands were replacing choirs in churches and "worship music" was replacing the traditional hymns of the faith, many who resisted the change cited the repetitious phrases of the new music as redundant and meaningless. In their opinion, repeating a phrase two dozen times, usually at the end of the song, reduced the depth of the character of worship. The music no longer held substance for them. However, when providing God-honoring, kingdom-seeking, biblically rooted leadership service, the character qualities of integrity, courage, and humility must be sung repetitiously. Just as the notes C, E, and G form a major chord pleasant to the ear, so integrity, courage, and humility are character qualities leaders need to compose the song of their leadership.

Integrity aligns our values, beliefs, and actions, creating a wholeness in which who we are and what we do are completely congruent. Under any circumstance, regardless of the consequences, you honor your commitments, live your convictions, and cultivate honesty and truthfulness. You practice what you preach and preach what you believe. The private you and the public you are one. As the saying goes, integrity means doing the right thing, even when no one else is there to judge. When composing the song of your life and leadership, the basic chord must harmonize without a note of hypocrisy. US senator Alan K Simpson said it best when introducing Gerald Ford at Harvard: "If you have integrity, nothing else matters. If you don't have integrity, nothing else matters."[23]

Courage is the willingness to act, embracing the risk, often in the face of opposition, and never giving up. Fear of failure, fear of taking a risk, and fear of what others might think of you are like adding a minor note to a major chord. When uncertainty, doubt, and fear play their dirges in your head, dispel them with a tune of courage by moving closer to that which you fear most. This is one way to tend to your heart, by cultivating courage deep in your soul. As Franklin D. Roosevelt once said, "Courage is not the absence of fear, but rather the assessment that something else is more important than fear."[24]

Humility is an attitude that demonstrates an inner quality of self-confidence with an outward expression of worthiness. Humble

CHAPTER SEVEN

people think more of others than of themselves, accept responsibility rather than assessing blame, and refrain from boasting about their accomplishments. They have a quiet, calm determination that demonstrates modesty and does not draw attention to themselves. Do not confuse their meekness with weakness. Humility is strength under control.

Integrity, courage, and humility demonstrate the basic form for leadership character. An example of basic form in music is the first movement in Beethoven's Fifth Symphony, which is built off a rhythmic motif of three eighth notes and a half note. In the same way, integrity, courage, and humility are the basic form of leadership used in composing your song. Composing your leadership song around these three notes creates a harmonious sound that is pleasant to the ear and lifts the spirits of those enjoying the music of your life.

> **KINGDOM TAKEAWAY**
>
> List characteristics of who you are. How are these characteristics reflected in your leadership actions? If a musical piece was composed of your leadership, what would it sound like?

CHAPTER EIGHT
PLAYING YOUR SONG

> *... speaking to one another with psalms, hymns, and songs from the Spirit. Sing and make music from your heart to the Lord ...*
> **Ephesians 5:19**

> *Do to others as you would have them do to you.*
> **Luke 6:31**

> *Musicians have their instruments. Engineers have their computers. Accountants have their calculators. Leaders have themselves. They are their own instruments.*
> **James M. Kouzes and Barry Z. Posner,**
> *The Five Practices of Exemplary Leadership*

> *Leadership is not wielding authority—it is empowering people.*
> **Attributed to Becky Brodin**

Leaders set the tone of the organizations they lead. Personality and persona, competence and character all are ingredients to communicating your voice and setting the tone of your leadership. Who you are—your strengths, values, and behavioral characteristics—

CHAPTER EIGHT

creates the song people will hear. How you communicate, relate to people, and approach your work are the notes on the soundtrack of your leadership. When you take action, the notes become the music that establishes the voice and tone of your leadership.

The power of this was driven home to me early in my presidency. Because of bad weather, the moving van did not arrive with our clothes in time for my first day on the job. So, I bought a corduroy jacket, dress pants, and a polo shirt to wear on my first day on campus as president, when I was to address an all-employee gathering. I was intentional in looking relaxed and wanted to identify as one of them. A couple of months into my tenure, while walking across campus, I met one of the campus leaders. We stopped and chatted for a while. As we were about to part, he casually mentioned, "Thank you for relaxing the dress code on campus." I had not rewritten any policy, sent out any email, or even discussed employee dress. But just by how I had dressed on the first day on the job, I had sent a message to the entire campus.

Leaders, intentionally or unintentionally, set the voice, tone, and mood of the organization. Like different genres of music, leaders have a personal soundtrack that permeates the entire organization. If you could name a song that would constantly play throughout the organization you are leading, what would it be? Do people hear your leadership as "Flight of the Bumblebee"? Or is it more like "Stars and Stripes Forever"? How about "Whiskey in the Jar"? Or "Moonlight Sonata"? Or maybe "The Impossible Dream"? Think music, not words. Who you are creates the song that everyone hears.

German composer Robert Schumann wrote much of his music to portray literary and imaginary characters and some real-life people. Most of his compositions have extramusical connections. Papillons, Op. 2, is based on literary characters, but some of his compositions are based on stories he made up himself. Carnaval, Op. 9, is the most descriptive of characters of any of his works.[25] If he could compose a musical piece portraying your leadership, how would it sound?

Personal soundtracks are created from your heart and soul combined with your style and work ethic. The concert heard by the stakeholders is communicated on the sound waves of emotional intelligence, response to crisis, and strategic implementation of vision.

Emotional intelligence is understanding yourself and the impact your emotions have on others while at the same time identifying how others are feeling and what they will need to become engaged. Max DePree describes the art of leadership as "liberating people to do what is required of them in the most effective and humane way possible."[26] Effective leadership is by nature relational. Leadership is an encounter between two or more individuals. A leader is someone you will follow to a place you could not or would not go by yourself. The very nature of leadership requires a situation that needs to be addressed, a person who is called to address it, and a group of people who are willing to become equipped and inspired for the common good. Your emotions and those of the stakeholders are the notes of the soundtrack you are playing.

How a leader deals with a crisis creates a song that multiple stakeholders hear in their heads. When a leader simply *reacts*, the music becomes dissonant, edgy, and intense. When a leader first gives the matter some thought and then *responds*, the song that is heard is one of strength, harmony, and progress. The song of the leader in crisis is often a "worm song"—the melody worms its way into your psyche and plays repeatedly all day long. How a leader is perceived as handling a crisis depends on how those impacted by the crisis remember what they heard.

Leadership by nature is visionary. Creating a compelling vision complete with effective strategies is music to the stakeholder's ears. Like an orchestra conductor who lifts his or her hands and unites the sounds of the many instrumentalists, so a leader unites the people around a shared vision and fills the air with music.

Knowing who you are—your persona and your leadership style—make up the soundtrack of your leadership. At the core of leadership is relationships. The musical chords played in the soundtrack of your leadership reveal how you treat people.

People like to be treated with respect, dignity, and value. I carry in my pocket a one-dollar gold coin to remind me to continually practice the golden rule in all my relationships. In all circumstances, whether having a hard conversation, making a purchase at a store, waiting in a customer service line, meeting with a close friend, or responding to criticism, I want to treat people as I would want to be treated in the same situation. The same is true in work relationships. Treating each person, be it a peer, a direct report, or the person I report to, as I want to be treated, given the situation, leads to a healthy work environment. Even when delivering bad news, confronting someone, or communicating termination of employment, I want to do so in the way I would want to be treated if I were the recipient of the communication. Practicing the golden rule does not mean you never have hard conversations, never issue ultimatums, and never practice tough love. What it does mean is that whatever the circumstance, you treat the person the way you would want to be treated in that situation. As a good friend remarked when we were discussing servanthood, "I do not mind being a servant. I just hate being treated like one." Practicing the golden rule honors people, treats them humanely, and serves them with humility and strength.

Sam Walton is reported to have said, "Outstanding leaders go out of their way to boost the self-esteem of their personnel. If people believe in themselves, it's amazing what they can accomplish."[27] When a person is appreciated, trusted, and affirmed, he or she responds with increased effort and productivity. A person who feels appreciated will almost always do more than what is expected. When a team trusts the person ultimately responsible for the outcome, the result is a group of high achievers influencing the outcomes of the organization. As Benjamin Franklin once said, "Well done is better than well said."[28]

Living and leading by the golden rule increases your integrity. Credibility, trust, and confidence are demonstrated by practicing the golden rule. Treating people well is a reflection on our character and influences others toward loyalty and commitment. Integrity motivates others to take responsibility and instills trust, which leads to greater effectiveness.

The coin in my pocket has two sides. One side reminds me to practice the golden rule. The flip side reminds me to remain committed to the gold standard. Often, practicing the golden rule carries with it a connotation of weakness, mediocrity, or people-pleasing. The gold standard is excellence, and effective leadership equips and inspires people to strive for excellence in all they do. Establishing high standards, measuring success, and holding people accountable are part and parcel of excellence.

Excellence enhances your influence. When Olympic athletes compete, they always "go for the gold." The initial dream, followed by disciplined training, final preparation, and then the competition itself, all have one goal in mind: to win a gold medal. Each event has only one winner. When the apostle Paul implored his readers to "run in such a way as to get the prize" (1 Corinthians 9:24), he was exhorting them to excellence and the gold standard. The athletes who are interviewed, who receive the attention, and who sign the lucrative endorsement contracts are the ones who have won the gold medals. Suddenly, their voices are heard, their influence is expanded, and they gain a large following. When one attains the gold standard, influence and leadership opportunities increase and the capacity to influence increases too. Excellence enhances influence.

Both sides of the gold coin are important. In some ways, these two sides of the coin are a paradox. When the apostle Paul stated that we are "to do . . . all in the name of the Lord Jesus" (Colossians 3:17), he was calling us to a life of excellence. The drive to succeed, the will to accomplish, and the commitment to excellence can easily get in the way of treating people humanely.

When Jesus made the statement we now call the golden rule, he did it in the context of how we are to treat our enemies. Leadership always has its detractors and critics. When a leader has the ability and the right to act (power and authority), it is all too easy to devalue and disrespect those he or she serves. Pursuing strategic objectives and implementing tactical plans coupled with a desire for excellence in all things can take precedence over practicing the emotional intelligence needed to move an organization forward. Treating those who

CHAPTER EIGHT

are not supportive of your leadership with dignity and respect is at the heart of the golden rule. As Dave Willis says, "Show respect even to people who don't deserve it, not as a reflection of their character, but as a reflection of yours."[29] This is the true meaning of the golden rule.

In many ways, practicing the golden rule and a commitment to the gold standard is more than actions, attitudes, and emotional intelligence. Together they can become a way of life, a mindset, and an organization's corporate culture. When a group earns a reputation for practicing the golden rule and a commitment to the gold standard, their vision becomes reality and their mission is accomplished almost naturally.

Valuing others more than yourself, striving continually to do more, and treating people with dignity and respect are the tones that compose the soundtrack of God-honoring, kingdom-seeking, biblically rooted leadership.

> **KINGDOM TAKEAWAY**
> How would you describe your leadership style? What is the voice, tone, and mood of your leadership? Identify ways you practice the "Golden Rule" in your leadership.

CHAPTER NINE
DANCING TO THE MUSIC

David and all Israel were celebrating with all their might before the LORD, with castanets, harps, lyres, timbrels, sistrums and cymbals.
2 Samuel 6:5

Let your conversation be always full of grace, seasoned with salt, so that you may know how to answer everyone.
Colossians 4:6

If you want to build a ship, don't drum up people to collect wood and don't assign them tasks and work, but rather teach them to long for the endless immensity of the sea.
Attributed to Antoine de Saint-Exupéry

    I grew up in a religious denomination in which dancing was considered a sin. Consequently, my feet have never been good at movement when music is played. As a church planter in Houston, Texas, I mentioned this belief during a Bible study. I was met with questioning looks. Nobody there had ever heard of such lunacy. I immediately realized I did not have any rationale to explain what I had been taught over the years.

CHAPTER NINE

A dozen years later, our daughter wanted a dance as part of her wedding reception, including the dance of the bride with her father. The night before the rehearsal, we moved back all the furniture in our family room, and she and I practiced the Texas two step. I learned how to move my feet by repeating in my head the phrase "quick quick slow slow" and counting "123-5 123-5." I was ready to dance with my daughter. When the time arrived, I proudly walked onto the dance floor, kissed the bride, and danced at her wedding. It was horrible. I was so focused on "quick quick slow slow . . . 123-5 123-5" that I was not enjoying the dance, plus my feet were not doing what they were supposed to do. I said to my daughter, "Let's forget the step and the counting. Let's just dance. This is the only time I will ever dance with the apple of my eye. Let's just dance." She threw back her head with a big laugh (which the photographer caught) and we just danced free form, loving every minute of it. Many fathers know the special relationship dads have with their daughters. The wedding dance is one of those special moments all dads cherish.

I wonder if the heavenly Father feels similarly when we honor his call, participate with him in his activity in the world, and see his mission become more of a reality. Participating with him in making his world the way he intended it to be brings joy to the Father's heart.

Dancing is a universal expression of music, usually celebratory in nature. All cultures and subcultures have a dance genre that expresses the music of their respective communities. From swing to disco, ceremonial dancing to street dancing, and from rhythm dancing to social dancing, celebrating the accomplishments of a group on mission places a song in the heart and joy in the steps of those involved. Equipping and inspiring a group of people to engage in seeing a vision become reality for the common good and enjoying the favor of God on their work is worthy of a celebration.

In 1966, the college I served as president was told that an auditorium would be built. Land on campus was designated. The board had named the auditorium. Two attempts at a capital campaign to fund it had failed. The people had all but given up. After a pre-campaign study, it was determined that the constituency still wanted an auditorium. In 2011 we launched a campaign to raise the needed funds to build a center for the arts. Many voices kept telling us we would fail. Discerning the voices through the five filters (mission, vision, values, resources, and Voice of One) influenced me to move forward with the project. By God's grace, the sacrificial giving of the Tabor College constituents, and the hard work of many people, in December 2017 we celebrated with a huge dedication weekend the likes of which the college had never experienced. Alumni and friends of the college came from across the nation to celebrate. The Shari Flaming Center for the Arts and Richert Auditorium were dedicated debt-free. Like King David of Israel, we celebrated with all our might before the Lord with an orchestra of instruments that affirmed a symphony of leadership to a packed house. As Methodist bishop Hanford Luccock says, "No one can whistle a symphony. It takes an orchestra to play it."[30]

Dancing to music is the natural response when people experience the thrill of accomplishment. "The ability to find one's voice and to hear and call other voices into harmonious sound," including identifying the Voice of One, is the magnum opus of any leader.[31]

Leadership is "being" resulting in "doing." Who a person is determines how that person leads, and how a person leads flows from who that person is. The soundtrack of our being and the actions of our doing make up the music people hear when we lead. When God smiles down on our leadership activity, the people break out in dancing.

Within two years of assuming the pastorate of a small church in western Kansas, we had grown to where we needed a new sanctuary. Plans were made, funding was secured, and a new sanctuary was built. On dedication weekend, as I was walking up the stairs, the person walking beside me, with a big smile on his face, said, "We did it, Pastor." What struck me was that the individual speaking had not been deeply involved in any aspect of the planning and construction process, and his financial contribution was minimal. Yet, when we celebrated, he felt like an integral part of the accomplishment. Celebrating successes, large and small, communicates appreciation, affirmation, and a sense of belonging.

Each dance style has signature moves. The tango has the open step, the forward cross, and the back cross. Ballet has the plié, etendre, glisser, relever, sauter, tourner, and elancer. The waltz performs

CHAPTER NINE

six steps known as the box step. Salsa has a pattern of six steps over eight counts of music. Square dancers listen to the caller for "circle left," "allemande left," "do-si-do," "right and left grand," "promenade," "swing," "roll away to a half sashay," and "ladies in, men sashay." Tap has ball heel, brush, shuffle, ball change, and flap. These signature moves of each respective dancing style are basic to learning and doing the dance well.

Dance moves erupt like attitudes. They are an expression of our thinking and feeling in response to what is happening in our lives and leadership. God-honoring, kingdom-seeking, biblically rooted leadership has basic moves that produce effective leadership. Three basic attitudes of effective leadership are gratitude, generosity, and graciousness.

Gratitude is an attitude, a choice we make regardless of our circumstances. In my observation, most Americans choose not to be grateful. When we make demands, think people owe us something, and work hard for what we receive, it is hard to be thankful. When we are arrogant, think we know best, and see ourselves better than others, it is hard to be thankful. When we are critical, judgmental, and negative about situations around us, it is hard to be thankful. Choosing gratitude happens when we value people, understand life as a stewardship given to us, and practice generosity.

Jesus was traveling through a small town when he encountered ten men who were dressed in rags. They smelled terrible from months of not bathing, their flesh was decaying, and they yelled "Unclean!" as they walked past others. They had leprosy, a flesh-eating disease. When they saw Jesus, the leprous men yelled, "Jesus have pity on us!" Jesus responded, "Go show yourselves to the priest!" The command made no sense to them, but what did they have to lose? So off they went. Suddenly all that leprosy had taken from them was restored. Fingers, ears, noses. They no longer had the disease. Can you imagine their response? "Let's go shopping and get some new clothes. Let's go home and hug our families. We are clean!" (Luke 17:11–19.) Now let me ask you: What would have been your response if this had happened to you? Of the ten men, only one, the one from a marginalized community, took the time to go back to Jesus and thank him. The nine others never did. Why would someone whose life was restored not return and thank the One who had given him new life?

This is a picture of our current society. I find that about 10 percent of people are genuinely thankful. As a college president, I often gave gifts to groups of people: Christmas gifts, beginning-of-academic-year gifts, bonuses, pay raises, rewards, accomplishment parties, victory parties, and tickets to events. I noticed that only about one in ten of them went out of their way to thank me for the gift by writing a personal note, sending a text, emailing, or making a phone call.

Gratitude, like a dance move, is central to effective leadership. If choosing to have an attitude of gratitude is difficult for you, and you want to learn the dance move of gratitude, begin by keeping a daily gratitude journal. Focus on what you have rather than what you do not have. Each day list one thing you are thankful for that day. By focusing on what God has given you, an attitude of gratitude will follow. You see, gratitude is not about what is going on in your life but what is going on in your mind.

Gratitude leads to **generosity**. On a trip to India, I was asked to speak at a church plant. The audience members were all at the bottom of the caste system and considered untouchables. They lived in lean-to shacks just outside a spice factory, where they worked. I had planned to speak on Jesus feeding the five thousand. But when I saw the crowd, I realized that this was not a relevant text. They were hungry, and unless I could produce food for them, the message would have no meaning. So, while they sang, I switched texts and preached on Zacchaeus, who was also an untouchable but whom Jesus did not pass by. (I left out the fact that he was a rich untouchable.)

After the service, people pressed in on us and wanted to be touched by us and receive a blessing. Jesus had been presented to them as a white person, and they were untouchables. Being touched by a white person was meaningful to these untouchables. So, I laid my hand on them and spoke a word of blessing. They in turn made a gesture of thanks. One lady, very poor, came up to me and pushed something into my Bible. Our eyes met, and she made a gesture of gratitude. I looked and discovered ten rupee, or a half day's wage, in my Bible. I asked my interpreter what I should do. He said, "Take it. She wants you to have it. Not taking it will insult her." I had thousands of rupees in my pocket. She had none. Yet she wanted me to have it. To this day, that ten rupee is still in my Bible at the exact place she placed it. Someone who had every reason not to be thankful demonstrated both gratefulness and generosity.

Being generous is an attitude witnessed in our actions. Giving of our time, treasure, and talent is living life in the stewardship entrusted to us by God. Generosity begins by recognizing that everything we have and are belongs to God. We live and give in response to God. We are happiest and must fulfilled when we give. And we are most like God when we are generous. God's model of generosity toward us sparks our motivation to be generous to others.

Angel, must I give again,
I ask in dismay.
And must I keep giving,
And giving and giving it away?
Oh no, said the angel,
His glance pierced me through.
Just keep giving
'Til the Lord stops giving to you.[32]

When we answer the call of the Voice of One for leadership service, bringing together a group of people to engage in participating with God's mission in the world, the leadership dance move of generosity is essential. Giving ourselves away in service; sharing our wealth, no matter how much or how little we have; and investing in the lives of the people in our care is a dance move that brings joy to all who are engaged in the symphony of praise that your leadership is creating.

It almost goes without saying that when you practice gratitude and generosity, your life is one of **graciousness**. Like generosity, graciousness is an attitude seen in our actions. It does not mean you are weak, indecisive, or without focus. Rather, it demonstrates your commitment to the value of everyone, affirms each person for his or her contribution, and deals with failures graciously yet firmly. Following the first two messages Jesus gave, one in the synagogue in Nazareth and one in Capernaum, his words were described as *gracious* and *with authority* (Luke 4:22, 36). Practicing graciousness is not a sign of weakness but strength when integrity, humility, and courage are the character qualities demonstrated by the gracious person. Simple leadership service actions, like remembering people's names, holding doors open, listening carefully, admitting you are wrong, practicing random acts of kindness, and asking questions of understanding, demonstrate an attitude of graciousness.

The attitudes of gratitude, generosity, and graciousness are three dance moves of leadership service that result in a life well lived.

> **KINGDOM TAKEAWAY**
> What attitudes best characterize your leadership? Where have you demonstrated or where should you demonstrate gratitude, generosity, and graciousness?

CHAPTER TEN
CHOOSING YOUR GENRE

"Do not think that I have come to abolish the Law or the Prophets; I have not come to abolish them but to fulfill them."
Matthew 5:17

"For the Son of man came to seek and to the lost."
Luke 19:10

Music is a moral law. It gives soul to the universe, wings to the mind, flight to the imagination, and charm and gaiety to life and to everything.
Attributed to Plato

Music opens a path into the realm of silence. Music reveals the human soul in "stark nakedness" as it were, without the customary linguistic draperies.
Josef Pieper, Only the Lover Sings

What is your preferred style of music? Classical? Rock? Country? Jazz? R & B? Gospel? The airwaves are filled with a variety of musical genres. From folk to hip-hop, pop to easy listening, and metal to contemporary Christian, to name a few. I am a southern gospel quartet fan and believe Gaither Homecoming music is what will be played in heaven.

When it comes to leadership, like the various musical genres, there are leadership styles that define the attitudes, actions, and decisions of a leader. Although situations often dictate what style is required to lead a group forward, in the end, a leader's style is on display in the legacy he or she has lived and created.

Legacy is a popular word. A Google search reveals legacy banks, rehabilitation centers, auto dealerships, insurance companies, brokerage firms, legal services, Realtors, medical arts, nutrition advising, a software company, a logistics company, a musical theater, ministries, a worship center, churches, funeral homes, obituary websites, a movie title, a band, gifts, campaigns, and schools. I am sure there are more who have attached the term *legacy* to their respective establishment or service. The technical definition of *legacy* is something passed on, either a gift, an idea, or a reputation.

Leaders create legacies. The legacy of a leader is the difference you made that will last and the reputations you acquired along the way. In the first months of my presidential service, a retired president asked me what my legacy would be as president of the college. I secretly had given thought to it but did not expect to engage in conversation about it. It seemed prideful and selfish to think about a legacy. However, I soon realized that the legacy I wanted to leave was not about me but about what would happen to the college, which was more dependent on others than on me. I discovered that most leaders do think about their legacies, what they intend to leave behind and the influence they want to be remembered for in history.

What I discovered during my tenure are three different types of legacies for those who serve in C-level leadership positions: the legacy you desire to have; the legacy resulting from situations, crises, accomplishments, or failures and your involvement in them; and the legacy that over time is attached to you by those you serve. Each of these three legacies identifies you as history marches on. I also learned that living your legacy was the best way to create a lasting legacy.

The legacy you desire. I began my tenure as president of the college desiring to see growth, creativity, and sustainability as the outcomes of my leadership. I hoped that when my service was completed, there would be enrollment, endowment, programmatic, personnel, and facility growth. Although these things all happened, somehow, they are not considered my legacy.

The legacy attributed to you. Being a visionary leader with a creative, action-oriented style that engages people and is principle driven resulted in significant accomplishment along with some disruptive chaos and relational carnage. The improved curbside appeal of the campus along with several new buildings, numerous remodeling projects and plazas, and upgraded parking lots, created a whole new look and feel for the campus. Building a major signature building added to this legacy. Despite all the hard work of so many staff and vendors, the upgrade of the campus is attributed to my leadership. As far as I am concerned, I was simply there when it all happened, encouraging, directing, and delegating all that needed to happen. Others did the work as I watched and cheered.

The legacy attached to you. By the grace of God, the generosity of our people allowed the college to raise a lot of money to pay for all the above-mentioned projects and growth. During my tenure as the thirteenth president of the college, more money was given in most years than ever before. The bean counters reported that we had raised more money under my leadership than under any previous president. Again, I saw it as a generous constituency that affirmed the projects we engaged in and graciously gave to see their school fulfill its mission. Staff, coaches, faculty, and students all participated in fundraising activities. However, the legacy attached to me by the people was that I am a fundraiser. No mother holding her newborn baby prays that he or she grow up to be a fundraiser. Yet I learned that it is a noble profession, helping people give meaning to their money by fulfilling the mission of God in his world.

Every leader leaves a legacy. Most want to leave a legacy. Few leave the legacy they wanted to leave. In the end, the legacy you lived is the legacy that lasts. Your everyday decisions, actions, and attitudes create your legacy. Legacies come from doing and being the leader God called you and arranged for you to be. As I reflect on my leadership service to the college, I realize that I lived my legacy day to day. My attitudes, actions, decisions, and relationship resulted in a style that became my reputation and mode of operation. While daily fulfilling the responsibilities of the role and office of president, I did not think about legacy. The mission, vision, values, and resources to fulfill the mission was what drove me to lead. My commitment to excellence and living the golden rule were what were on my mind. Living and leading in a God-honoring, kingdom-seeking, biblically rooted way was my one desire. The Bible verses (Isaiah 30:21 and Proverbs 16:9) impressed upon my mind the first day I walked onto the campus as president were my constant guide. They defined the style I wanted to demonstrate and communicate.

When you consider the life of Jesus, you find these three types of legacies. In the Gospels, the legacy Jesus desired was to preach the kingdom of God (Luke 4:43). When John the Baptist was sitting in prison and entertaining doubts, he sent two of his disciples to ask Jesus if he was the Messiah. Jesus' response was, "Report . . . what you have seen and heard" (Luke 7:22). Jesus' first sermons recorded in Luke 4, probably the shortest sermon on record, reveals his desired legacy: "Today this scripture is fulfilled in your hearing" (v. 21). The scripture he had read was Isaiah 61:1–2, announcing that he would preach good news to the poor, proclaim freedom for the prisoners and recovery of sight for the blind, release the oppressed, and "proclaim the year of the Lord's favor" (Luke 4:18–19). These actions are kingdom actions characterizing the life of Jesus while living on earth.

The legacy attributed to Jesus was as a disrupter of the religious practices of the Jewish people. Throughout his life, the religious leaders of the time rejected his ministry, calling it demonic; criticized his actions of healing on the Sabbath and his hanging out with those on the margins; and accused him of blasphemy when he forgave sins and indirectly claimed he was the Son of God.

However, the legacy attached to him down through the ages is that he was and remains the savior of the world. His death and resurrection once and for all cemented into history that he came to seek and save those who were lost. The message of the salvation he brings for all humankind has been proclaimed throughout the world.

If there is any doubt regarding Jesus' legacy, look at the Gospels, where he stated why he came to earth (emphasis added):

"Do not think that I have *come* to abolish the Law or the Prophets; I have not *come* to abolish them but to fulfill them."
Matthew 5:17

"But go and learn what this means: 'I desire mercy, not sacrifice.' For I have not *come* to call the righteous, but sinners."
Matthew 9:13

"Do not suppose that I have *come* to bring peace to the earth. I did not *come* to bring peace, but a sword. For I have *come* to turn 'a man against his father, a daughter against her mother, a daughter-in-law against her mother-in-law.'"
Matthew 10:34–35

"The Son of Man did not *come* to be served, but to serve, and to give his life as a ransom for many."
Matthew 20:28

"Jesus replied, 'Let us go somewhere else--to the nearby villages--so I can preach there also. That is why I have *come*.'"
Mark 1:38

"On hearing this, Jesus said to them, 'It is not the healthy who need a doctor, but the sick. I have not *come* to call the righteous, but sinners.'"
Mark 2:17

"For even the Son of Man did not *come* to be served, but to serve, and to give his life as a ransom for many."
Mark 10:45

"I have not *come* to call the righteous, but sinners to repentance."
Luke 5:32

"For the son of man *came* to seek and to save the lost."
Luke 19:10

"I have _come_ in my Father's name, and you do not accept me; but if someone else comes in his own name, you will accept him."
John 5:43

"All that the Father gives me will come to me, and whoever comes to me I will never drive away. For I have _come_ down from heaven not to do my will but to do the will of him who sent me."
John 6:37–38

"Jesus said to them, 'If God were your Father, you would love me, for I have _come_ here from God. I have not come on my own; God sent me.'"
John 8:42

Jesus said, "For judgment I have _come_ into this world, so that the blind will see and those who see will become blind."
John 9:39

"The thief comes only to steal and kill and destroy; I have _come_ that they may have life, and have it to the full."
John 10:10

"I have _come_ into the world as a light, so that no one who believes in me should stay in darkness. If anyone hears my words but does not keep them, I do not judge that person. For I did not _come_ to judge the world, but to save the world."
John 12:46–47

Today if you would ask people what kind of person Jesus was, descriptive words like *kind, compassionate, forgiving, accepting,* and *loving* would be the terms associated with him. Yet *those* who have heard his voice, opened the door, and invited him in would describe him as *Lord, Savior,* and *Friend* (see (Revelation 3:20). Together these descriptions create the legacy of Jesus.

The genre of your leadership becomes your legacy. Living it each day creates a style that worms its way into the minds and hearts of the people in your care and cements their view of you down through history. Practicing what you learned in God's music school, composing your own song, and playing it with gusto while dancing to the

CHAPTER TEN

music of your leadership comes together in a genre for all to hear and remember.

> **KINGDOM TAKEAWAY**
>
> How do you want to be remembered? What situations are determining how you will be remembered? How is your leadership lifestyle influencing what others are experiencing and remembering?

CHAPTER ELEVEN

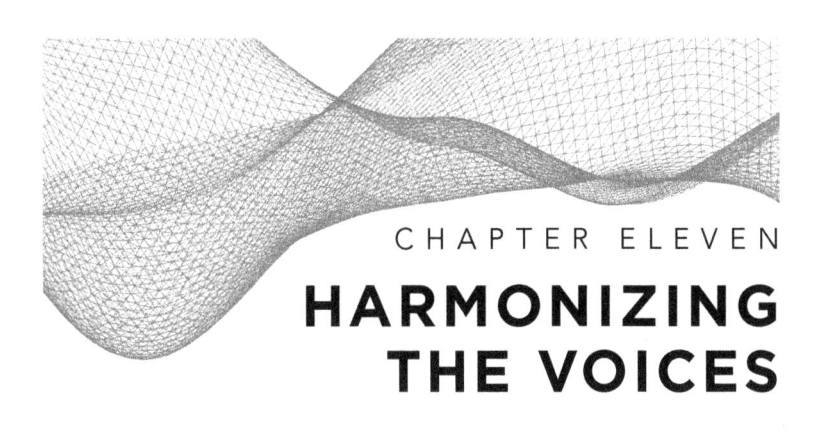

HARMONIZING THE VOICES

. . . singing psalms and hymns and spiritual songs among yourselves, and making music to the Lord in your hearts.
Ephesians 5:19 (NLT)

To build a strong team, you must see someone else's strength as a complement to your weakness and not a threat to your position or authority.
Attributed to Christine Caine

Great things in business are never done by one person, they're done by a team of people.
Attributed to Steve Jobs

The way a team plays as a whole determines its success. You may have the greatest bunch of individual stars in the world, but if they don't play together, the club won't be worth a dime.
Attributed to Babe Ruth

A good friend of mine tells the story of when he was in college and sang in the prestigious college concert choir. During a recording session, the director stopped and asked for a section of the choir to sing. After listening intently, he asked five of the choir members to sing. Then he asked two of them to sing. Finally, pointing to my friend, he said, "Don't sing quite so loudly." Evidently, my friend's voice was not what the director wanted to create a harmonious sound for the album.

The leader practicing the acoustical art of leadership is continually fine-tuning the sound for a harmonious rendition. Bringing together the many voices and creating a harmonious sound inspires both the people engaged in moving toward the preferred future and those experiencing the influence of those involved. The ability to depend on your direct reports to align in four-part harmony is built on the expectations outlined for the team. The four-part harmony of speaking the truth in love, embracing hard realities, entrusting responsibilities, and demonstrating loyalty creates a harmonious song.

A biblical example of bringing together a strong team is Jesus and the twelve individuals he chose as his apprentices. Their capacity, intelligence, and emotional maturity certainly can be called into question. None of them in his own right seemed to have leadership qualities that could bring together a group of people and lead them toward a preferred future for the common good. However, these unlikely candidates for world changers were called and responded to the master influencer himself to become a team to begin to fulfill the mission of God in the world. The attitude and actions of Jesus as he interacted with his apprentices, teaching them kingdom truths, demonstrated the qualities that create a harmonious sound.

Jesus **spoke the truth in love**. When the apprentices scolded the parents of little children who wanted to have Jesus bless them, his righteous anger showed, and he responded by speaking truth about the kingdom of God concerning who could gain membership and how (Mark 10:13–16).

When a wealthy person of authority asked a question about life in the hereafter and followed by telling Jesus how faultless a life he had lived, "Jesus looked at him and loved him," then broke the news to him that his wealth was in the way of his eternal life. Then, explaining to his apprentices the relationship between wealth and eternal life, Jesus again spoke truth to them (Mark 10:17–31).

When two of the apprentices asked for preferential treatment, Jesus calmly asked if they were up for the task. When the rest of the group showed their displeasure with the two who wanted special treatment, Jesus spoke the truth about status, expectations, and the reverse order of importance when following him (Mark 10:35–45).

Earlier, the apprentices were asked to heal a tormented child but they did not succeed. Jesus himself set the young boy free. When the apprentices asked why they had not been successful, Jesus spoke truth to them about what is needed to bring release from evil (Mark 9:14–32).

When Jesus was celebrating the Passover with the apprentices, he foretold that Peter would say he did not know Jesus. Peter vehemently assured Jesus he would remain true. Jesus' forth telling was correct, as always: Peter caved and proclaimed he had never known Jesus However, after Jesus' resurrection, at a cookout along the sea, Jesus took Peter aside and restored him by asking Peter three times if he still loved him. Jesus spoke the truth of love acceptance, and forgiveness to Peter and gave him an assignment for life (Mark 14:66–72; John 21:15–23).

Repeatedly, Jesus lovingly spoke truth to his apprentices, equipping and preparing them for their roles once he left earth. With kindness and firmness, he spoke truth into their lives, uniting them to fulfill his mission on earth.

While I served as president of a college, the executive team meetings could get quite heated. We had a culture of each person speaking his or her mind in an atmosphere of acceptance, challenge, and honesty. We were never left wondering what each team member thought or his or her stand on the issues being discussed. Truth telling with love brought us together as a team.

Jesus **embraced hard realities**. The entire time he traveled the countryside with his apprentices, Jesus was forewarning them about his impending suffering, death, and resurrection. Each of the writers telling the story of Jesus' time on earth communicated the many attempts Jesus made to inform and prepare his apprentices for his final days on earth, along with the meaning associated with and foretold by the prophets. He clearly and without mincing words embraced the hard realities of his last days. The writer Luke provides the clearest and most succinct description of Jesus' communication of the harsh realities he faced:

> Taking the twelve disciples aside, Jesus said, "Listen, we're going up to Jerusalem, where all the predictions of the prophets concerning the Son of Man will come true. He will be handed over to the Romans, and he will be mocked, treated shamefully, and spit upon. They will flog him with a whip and kill him, but on the third day he will rise again."
>
> But they didn't understand any of this. The significance of his words was hidden from them, and they failed to grasp what he was talking about. (Luke 18:31–34 NLT)

Talking about suffering and death is not easy, especially when discussing it with close friends and people you love and who love you. But Jesus did not shy away from explaining his death and resurrection to his team of apprentices.

Max Depree in *Leadership Is an Art* states, "The first responsibility of leadership is to define reality."[33] Often, defining the hard realities involves finances and personnel. Having the needed resources to accomplish the mission and making sure the right people are on the bus and in the right seats can create hard realities.

I assumed the college presidency during the Great Recession of 2008. During my second year we realized we would need to make some difficult decisions regarding the college. Specifically, we would need to reduce our payroll. Meeting after excruciating meeting, decisions were made, resulting in trimming our workforce by 11 percent. Before I made the final decisions, I took our plan to my predecessor and sought his counsel. Did we miss anything? Did we not think of something? Were there other options? He looked over the plan and replied, "This is what needs to be done . . ." I asked, "Why did you not do this when you were president?" He responded, "I did not have to. But now you do."

Implementing the decisions was even more difficult. Timelines and communications were clearly laid out as we prayed together, cried together, and planned together. I met those affected by the reduction privately in their respective offices. The pastors of those personnel were made aware of the impending news. This was one of the most difficult days of my presidency. Embracing hard realities is an important part of providing leadership. The experience brought our team together in incredible ways. Dealing with hard realities by speaking the truth in love creates harmony among the team.

Jesus **entrusted responsibilities** to his apprentices. While moving from town to town, proclaiming, healing, and delivering all who asked, Jesus realized that his impact could be multiplied. To expand his influence and provide the needed equipping and inspiration for his apprentices, he shared his authority with them and sent them out with instructions to proclaim, heal, and deliver. His instructions were visionary, precise, and thorough. When the men returned, they were pumped because they had experienced the joy and satisfaction of helping people experience the kingdom of God (Matthew 10; Luke 9).

During the time between Jesus' resurrection from the dead and his return to his heavenly home, Jesus continued to entrust responsibilities not only to his apprentices, but to all who would in the future choose to honor and follow him: "As the Father has sent me, I am sending you. And with that he breathed on them and said, 'Receive the Holy Spirit'" (John 20:21–22). His desire to see the world as he intended it to be is placed in the hands of those who choose to follow him.

People want to contribute to fulfilling the mission and seeing the vision become a reality. Nothing is more frustrating than unclear expectation, fuzzy outcomes, and a supervisor micromanaging your work. On one occasion, when one of my direct reports had dropped the ball big time, we discussed the consequences everyone would experience due to the breakdown. It was a sobering moment. Later that day I reflected on our conversation and realized I had not set a new direction. So, I wrote an email to the employee, clarifying the expectations and intended outcomes. I closed the email by communicating that he was responsible for the project, that the preferred future was clear, and that I would be there to support and encourage him to make it happen. Later he told me how much the email had meant to him. It had motivated him to give it his best because he was in charge, and it was his responsibility. He took ownership in a new way. Embracing hard realities while speaking the truth in love and demonstrating your confidence in those on the team by entrusting them with responsibility becomes a harmonious song the entire organization loves to hear.

Jesus required **loyalty**. He minced no words when calling people to him. His strongest words are found in Mark 8:34–35:

> If any of you wants to be my follower, you must give up your own way, take up your cross, and follow me. If you try to hang on to your life, you will lose it. But if you give up your life for my sake and for the sake of the Good News, you will save it (NLT).

Repeatedly he stated clearly and bluntly that he would not share allegiance with anyone or anything else. Jesus demanded loyalty even to the point of death.

The practice of the college's executive leadership team was to present a united front to the board of directors. During the team meeting, all sides of a matter were explored, usually with significant disagreement. But once a decision was made, I expected the team to move forward together. I expected loyalty, not to me but to the team. After one board meeting one of the members asked me if the executive leadership team ever disagreed. I laughed out loud as I explained to how much disagreement we experienced in our meetings. However, once a decision was made, we were united in moving forward.

Loyalty, truth telling, facing reality, and sharing responsibility create a harmonious sound that creates a corporate culture all enjoy.

Four-part harmony can be enhanced with skilled instrumentation. Like the tickling of the ivories while the singers sing, the practice of creativity and innovation enhances the sound. Jesus' creativity is seen in the many stories he told speaking the truth, embracing hard realities, entrusting responsibilities, and communicating the loyalty he demanded. Creativity produces new approaches, ideas, and actions. Innovation applies creativity to a specific context. All teams need creativity and innovation to address and solve the hard realities facing them. These two qualities need to be embedded in the culture, enabling the organization to fulfill its mission. When creativity and innovation permeate the team, the resulting song becomes an inspiration to all who are working to fulfill God's mission in the world.

Early in my church-planting days, I attended a pastor's seminar hosted by Rick Warren. At one point in his presentation, he quoted the following, which I typed up and attached to a blank page in my Bible as a reminder to me as we attempted to start a church.

Great People

Are ready to help me. At the right time. In the right way.

People I do not even know yet!

I promise: I'll never give up because I do not have the help.

But I will trust God to provide!

God has resources to help you that you have not even considered.

God will bring thousands of persons with all sorts of talents, skills, concerns, and contacts into your life in order to fulfill His plans. So, open your eyes and see the faces of people around you. Open your ears to hear what they are saying. Today, tomorrow, next week, you'll meet someone – someone who is just the person you need. That right person will come along to fill the right place at just the right time. And you will marvel knowing that God arranged it so beautifully!

> **KINGDOM TAKEAWAY**
>
> Identify the people that are serving with you in leading a group towards a preferred future. What characteristics do these people have in common?

CHAPTER TWELVE
SONGBOOK OF LEADERSHIP

You led your people like a flock by the hand of Moses and Aaron.
Psalm 77:20

And David shepherded them with integrity of heart; with skillful hands he led them.
Psalm 78:72

A theology is only as good as the implications that flow from it.
Jeffrey K. Salkin, Jewish Journal

If you don't listen to Theology, that won't mean that you have no ideas about God. It'll mean that you'll have a lot of wrong ones.
C. S. Lewis, Beyond Personality

I grew up in a church that sang the historic hymns of the faith along with gospel hymns. You could tell the difference by the time signatures. The historic hymns of the faith were usually written in 4/4 time while the gospel hymns were mostly written in 3/4 time. When I attended seminary, some professors taught that many of the hymns we sing are not good, sound theology. I was never bothered by that because the focus of my singing was, as the psalmist says, to "make a joyful noise unto the LORD" (Psalm 100:1 KJV).

The songbook of the ancient people of God was the Psalter. The Psalms, as we have come to know them, have a theology of their own. They offer praise and thanksgiving, encouragement, and consolation, and point us to a future and a hope. The Psalms are part of the inspired, infallible, inerrant, authoritative written Word of God. Creating a theology of leadership from the songbook of the people of God seems appropriate and leads to good, sound theology.

Like all theologies, this one is incomplete. However, the Psalms provide some compelling statements that communicate an understanding of leadership. They point to three theological truths: (1) God leads. (2) We are engaged in a holy partnership with God. (3) Our part of the partnership is to engage in the actions of listening, seeing, learning, doing, and loving. These three combined become the score on which the practice of leadership service is written and coordinated. A musical score allows one to see all the notes and how they all fit together. A theology of leadership serves as a score for all leadership activity.

Leadership is described in very simple terms in Psalm 78:72: "And David shepherded them with integrity of heart; with skillful hands he led them." Asaph, a worship leader for King David, composed a song describing the legacy influence of direction and provision the Lord had on his people down through the generations. But they refused to honor the Lord. Asaph's composition notes that "they continued to sin against him" (v. 17), resulting in the people's hopelessness and defeat. However, amid these multiple rejections, the Lord raised up David. The description of his leadership provides a foundational understanding of leadership. Leadership consists of *integrity of heart* and *skillful hands*. Who a person is and what a person does are the bass and treble clefs of the score. Leadership is being that results in doing. Who you are determines how you lead and how you lead flows from who you are.

The life and leadership of King David, the author of at least seventy-three of the psalms, defines the essence of leadership. He was a person of immense influence by both his example and his actions. He attracted high-capacity followers who fought, honored, and revered him. He was all-encompassing, someone the entire nation followed to places they could not or would not go by themselves. He equipped and inspired an entire nation to pursue a preferred future for the common good of all. As God's chosen one, he influenced the nation toward the purposes of God. Together they went to places where God wanted them to be and participated with him in his activity in the world. David was considered a "man after [God's] own heart" (Acts 13:22). His willingness to "do everything I want him to do" is a model of leadership for us today (v. 22b). His heart was in tune with God's heart as he honored the Lord's influence. The psalms he wrote became the basis of our theology of leadership from the songbook of the ancient people of God.

In exploring the psalms, we discover first and foremost that **God leads.** Fundamental to all kingdom-seeking, God honoring, biblically rooted leadership is the fact that God is the premier model of leadership. From the beginning of time, his influence is witnessed throughout the world he created.

In Psalm 104:27, the psalmist, after declaring praise to the Lord with a litany of what God has done in and for creation, makes a summary statement: "All creatures look to you [God] to give them their food at the proper time." Jesus referenced this psalm when talking about being ready when the end of time comes. He affirms readiness as an excellent stewardship practice of a wise and faithful servant (see Luke 12:40–42). The consummate leader, the Lord, models good stewardship for all of humankind as evidenced in his relationship to creation. In leadership terms, "do the right thing and do things right" is the stewardship of the Lord.

All of leadership is a stewardship placed in our hands by the Lord and those on earth who have given us the authority to lead. It is a stewardship of mission and vision, resources and relationships,

CHAPTER TWELVE

power and authority, time and talent, reputation and message, lives, and organizational culture. Every direction we set, every strategy we implement, and every decision we make is a stewardship entrusted to us to fulfill God's purposes on earth.

The Psalms also communicate the virtues of God's influence. Humility, doing right, and respect are highly esteemed by the master leader. Psalm 25:9–10 proclaims, "He leads the humble in doing right, teaching them his way. The LORD leads with unfailing love and faithfulness all who keep his covenant and obey his demands" (NLT). When we practice humility while setting things right, we experience his pleasure and participate in making the world as he intended it to be. Jim Collins in *Good to Great* calls it "Level 5" leadership when humility and fierce resolve come together.[34] These verses also describe someone who is both supportive and directive in his influence in our lives. God's compassion and understanding inspire us to serve, and when we need direction, he shows the way.

Central to the understanding of God's people is that he leads them. In Psalm 80:1 Asaph appeals to the Lord as the one who led the people centuries ago: "Hear us, Shepherd of Israel, you who lead Joseph like a flock. You who sit enthroned between the cherubim, shine forth." The entire deliverance experience from their oppressors is remembered as the Lord leading them. The cloud, the pillar of fire, and the journey were understood as the Lord leading them to a preferred future.

However, God's leadership is not done in a vacuum. He carries out his purposes on earth through those he calls, inspires, and equips to make the world as he intended it to be. **We are engaged in a holy partnership.** Kingdom-seeking leadership service is a holy partnership with the Lord himself.

Psalm 77:20 affirms both the leadership of God and his partnership with us: "You [God] led your people like a flock by the hand of Moses and Aaron." The rescue of the people from their oppressors was understood as the Lord leading through the activity of Moses and Aaron. Moses acted. Aaron spoke. And God led. A great demonstration of the holy partnership.

When I accepted the call to become a college president, the board formed a committee to plan an inauguration. Although I felt quite uncomfortable with the whole idea, I soon realized this was a rite of passage whose purpose was for the institution to celebrate its mission and affirm its vision. The theme the committee chose was "Called to Serve; Chosen to Lead." It struck a chord in my soul that remained for my tenure as president. Near the end of my time of service, I created a paperweight with this phrase etched into a stone, which I gave to those who had diligently worked with me in leading the college. Each of them was called to serve and had been chosen to lead. I challenged them to continue to lead well.

As I began to fulfill the responsibilities of the role, I quickly learned that everything I was engaged in as a president was not my doing, but the Lord's. We were partners in the pursuit of accomplishing the mission and vision of the college. The funds we raised, the buildings we built, the programs we implemented, the new business model we embraced, the rebranding of the institution—all were the results of the Lord moving hearts, uniting us in purpose and values, and inspiring us to give it our all. The transformation of lives, the preparation for meaningful vocations, and the inspiration to live a life of service were of no value if the Lord was not intimately and intricately involved in the process. In the midst of many accomplishments, I realized how true were the words of Solomon in Psalm 127:1: "Unless the LORD builds the house, the builders labor in vain. Unless the LORD watches over the city, the guards stand watch in vain." All the positive advances of the college were God's doing, and I was in partnership with him in moving the institution forward toward our preferred future.

Experiencing the outcomes of this holy partnership affirms what Psalm 115:16 proclaims: "The highest heavens belong to the LORD, but the earth he has given to mankind." Our role in the holy partnership is affirmed. We have been placed on this earth to influence.

CHAPTER TWELVE

As in all partnerships, each person has his or her role and assigned activity to make the partnership productive. In the holy partnership, **we engage in the leadership actions of listening, seeing, learning, doing, and loving.** The leadership actions of the holy partnership are like the diatonic musical scale described in chapter 1. Our responsibility is to listen, see, learn, do, and love. Let's look at each of these responsibilities individually:

Listening to the Lord. When engaged in kingdom-seeking, God-honoring, biblically rooted leadership, listening to the One who has called us into leadership service is essential as we influence people toward his purposes. The temple musician who wrote Psalm 85:8 affirms the importance of listening. After proclaiming the activity of God to his people and pleading for him to again intervene in their lives, he declares, "I will listen to what God the LORD says; he promises peace to his people, his faithful servants—but let them not turn to folly." If you want to be a part of God's activity in the world, listen to him.

Seeing the world as God sees it and recognizing his activity in the world. The psalmist offers up high praise, declaring the mightiness and awesomeness of the works of God and inviting us to "come and see what God has done, his awesome deeds for mankind!" (Psalm 66:5). When we are faced with difficult and perplexing situations, we often seek to understand them from a human perspective. When in a holy partnership, seeing the situation as God sees it can open up a whole new world of possibilities.

Learning from what we have heard and seen. Once we have heard what the Lord desires and seen the situation from his vantage point, we must then process and interpret all the information and learn from it. What we learn equips us for the task ahead. Often, we are shaped by the experience and we grow in character, capacity, and understanding. Once we have experienced the voice of the Lord and had our eyes opened to his ways, our hearts yearn for his understanding: "Show me your ways, LORD, teach me your paths. Guide me in your truth and teach me, for you are God my Savior, and my hope is in you all day long" (Psalm 25:4–5). When David wrote this song, he was pleading with the Lord to show him his favor.

Doing *the work.* Once we have heard from the Lord, seen the situation as he sees it, and learned from what he has shown us, it is time to *do*. Have the courage to take the needed action to address the situation that needs resolution. You have the responsibility to, as David wrote in Psalm 37:3, "Trust in the Lord and do good; dwell in the land and enjoy safe pasture." Leadership is an activity. Leaders are by nature action-oriented people. When the actions are inspired by what you have heard, seen, and learned, then the courage to take the needed actions are a natural result. When criticism comes, your confidence remains because you have listened, saw, and learned.

Loving *others.* Finally, in everything, practice love. Throughout the songbook, God's love for us is affirmed. In Psalm 136, every statement of thanksgiving, praise, and godly activity is antiphonally answered by the phrase "His love endures forever." When David fled from the pursuit of Saul, he proclaimed in Psalm 57:10, "For great is your love, reaching to the heavens; your faithfulness reaches to the skies." No matter what the circumstances, the love of God is always our experience. This deep and continual love is our inspiration to love others. Those whom the Lord has placed in our care as we fulfill his call to leadership service are motivated to engage as we love them. Rick Warren states it simply: "The first job of people is to love people. Leadership without love is manipulation."[35]

When we participate with the Lord in fulfilling his mission in the world, we are engaged in a holy partnership. This holy partnership is quite simplistic:

God speaks. We listen.

God does. We see.

God teaches (equips). We learn.

God inspires. We do.

God loves. We love.

CHAPTER TWELVE

When the complexities of leadership are brought together in one location, they are written on the score of "God leads." We are engaged in a holy partnership. And our leadership actions are to listen, see, learn, do, and love.

> **KINGDOM TAKEAWAY**
> What is your theology of leadership? Which biblical text(s) or story(ies) are the foundation of your theology of leadership?

NOISE

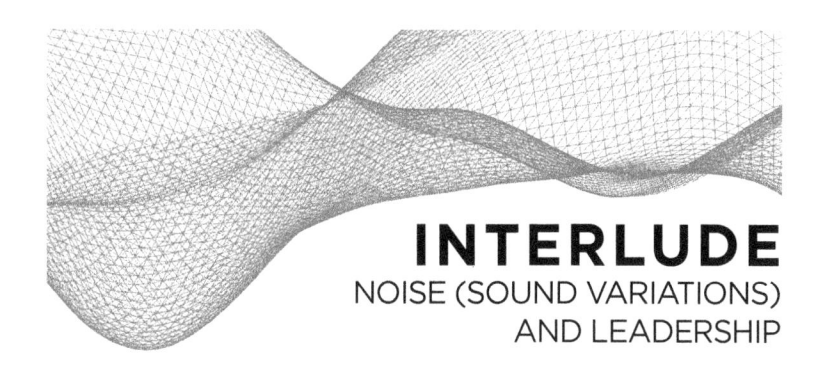

INTERLUDE
NOISE (SOUND VARIATIONS) AND LEADERSHIP

One Fourth of July together with my two adult sons, we went to a fireworks stand to purchase some fireworks. As my sons were perusing the options, Charlie, the stand owner, started pitching the item my sons were considering. "That one has a nice *pow* at the bottom and a loud *boom* on top." We bought it, laughed about it on the way to the car, and later that evening lit it. None of us remember what it looked like, but we remember how Charlie had described it. "Nice *pow* on the bottom and large *boom* on top." Why do we remember what we heard instead of what we saw? And what is the difference between a "pow" and a "boom"?

Noise is simply a vibration that travels through a medium. How we perceive it determines what kind of noise it is. Four types of noise are *continuous noise, intermittent noise, impulsive noise,* and *low-frequency noise*. Some noises are unwanted, unpleasant, and disruptive. Others are welcomed, soothing, and desirable. Our perception is the determining factor.[36]

Leadership in the same way is perceived in different ways. Some perceive it as command and control. Others perceive it as power and position. And some perceive it as surrender and service. Like a vibration, leadership travels through a medium and is perceived in a variety of ways. All these leadership variations, like noise, make an impact on the hearer. They invade our psyche and reverberate through our lives, either inspiring and equipping or discouraging and destroying us. Leadership can be life-giving or life-diminishing.

CHAPTER TWELVE

How leadership is perceived and how one responds are determined by both the one influencing and the one being influenced.

> **KINGDOM TAKEAWAY**
> How do you perceive leadership?

CHAPTER THIRTEEN
SOUND FREQUENCIES

> *"You know that those who are regarded as rulers of the Gentiles lord it over them, and their high officials exercise authority over them. Not so with you. Instead, whoever wants to become great among you must be your servant, and whoever wants to be first must be slave of all. For even the Son of Man did not come to be served, but to serve, and to give his life as a ransom for many."*
> **Mark 10:42–45**

> *He who does not desire power is fit to hold it.*
> **Attributed to Plato**

> *Leadership is like beauty: it's hard to define, but you know it when you see it.*
> **Warren Bennis,** *On Becoming a Leader*

Sound is measured by frequency and intensity. Frequency, commonly known as *pitch*, is measured by hertz (Hz) and is the total number of waves produced in a second. Intensity is measured by decibels (dB) and is the perceived loudness of the sound. When we hear a sound, these two measuring units help us interpret what we

CHAPTER THIRTEEN

are hearing. Yet each person hears and interprets sound differently. To one, the sound may seem loud and obnoxious while to another the sound may seem normal and inspiring. Jimmy Hendrix's rendition of "The Star Spangled Banner" at Woodstock was deeply appreciated. Some today say it is one of the best renditions of our national anthem ever heard. Yet for others, it was anything but patriotic and is heard as disrespectful and unpatriotic.

In my interview with the board of directors of the college, I asked what they wanted in a president. Various answers were given as to what they thought a president should be and do. They offered no clear and concise statement of what the expectations were of me and the role. After some time, the board chair summarized the answers. "What we are saying is that we want someone to make the college work. We will know it when we see it. Take us to the next level." I smiled and accepted this as a green light to lead as I wanted to lead. Fourteen years later, at my retirement, this same group affirmed that the college was in a better place, and we had moved to the next level. In an elusive way, they measured leadership.

Evaluating leadership is as much art as it is science. Our common experience tells us that some naturally have a capacity to rally a group toward a preferred future. All the qualities seem there organically to influence and succeed. Analytics of all kinds are available to assess the effectiveness of leaders while learning how to increase one's effectiveness. From ROI (return on investment) to KPI (key performance indicators), from EQ (emotional intelligence quotient) to IQ (intelligence quotient), and from SLII (Situational Leadership II) to the LPI (Leadership Practices Inventory), productivity and leadership characteristics of a leader can be measured. Dozens of cottage industries have sprung up around a variety of assessments.[37]

Like sound frequency and intensity, leadership is interpreted in many ways. The media—social media in particular—interpret leadership activities according to their own agendas. Sadly, the airwaves and media are full of less-than-stellar stories of "Christian" leaders whose attitudes and actions seem to defy what it means to be Christian. When one examines these leadership activities, distinguishing them from normal marketplace leadership actions is difficult. The rhetoric, metrics, and strategies seem to mirror the marketplace leadership activity, with the only difference being the intended mission or desired outcomes.

We all recognize natural normal leadership when we see it in the marketplace. But what is the difference between marketplace leadership and kingdom-seeking, God-honoring, biblically rooted leadership? How does kingdom leadership reflect the King? How does one evaluate if leadership brings satisfaction and joy to the heavenly Father? What are the leadership frequencies that communicate God-honoring leadership?

At the heart of distinguishing marketplace leadership from kingdom leadership are the motivations of the leader. My observations have led to the conclusion there are four differing leadership motivations.

In self-driven leadership, a person is driven by his or her own capabilities and ego. Examples are abundant. In principle-driven leadership, a person and group identify a set of principles, and the company or organization live these out in a fierce and loyal way. Values-driven corporations are examples. In purpose-driven leadership, a person and organization are committed solely to the mission of the organization. Most nonprofit groups are examples of this motivation. In kingdom-driven leadership a person is driven by a phrase from what we know as the Lord's Prayer: "Your kingdom come, your will be done, on earth as it is in heaven" (Matthew 6:10). I am convinced that kingdom leadership is the motivation that brings joy to the Father.

Three leadership frequencies best identify the kingdom leadership paradigm:

Frequency #1. Kingdom leaders seek God's kingdom rather than build their own empire.

Leaders are by nature builders. "Leaders think and act at the intersection of two axes: the first, between the past and the future;

the second, between the abiding values and aspirations of those they lead."[38] When a person senses God's call to participate with him in his mission in the world by addressing a situation, the normal response is to begin building. We want to see God's kingdom on earth established, so we marshal the resources to build his kingdom. We plan, organize, and implement strategies to advance the kingdom of God. Our efforts are to grow whatever ministry we are called to with the intended purpose of increasing the influence of God in the world. We establish systems, procedures, and policies that build the organization so the kingdom of God can advance and multiply its influence. Often, the metrics used to evaluate the effectiveness of the ministry are the same as any marketplace organization would use.

However, no place in Scripture are we asked to build God's kingdom. In the Gospels, the verbs associated with the kingdom of God are "enter," "receive," "seek," "preach, "proclaim," "inherit," and "waiting."[39] We enter the kingdom as recipients and seek it by preaching and proclaiming its good news, waiting for God's rule in all its fullness. We are called to "seek first his kingdom and his righteousness, and all these things will be given to you as well" (Matthew 6:33). Normal, natural leadership builds empires. Kingdom leaders seek to proclaim the activity of the king. Leadership in the kingdom continually seeks, proclaims, and waits for the work of God in the world to be realized. When Luke wrote the Acts of the Apostles, he described the apostles' activity using the same words and added "arguing," "explaining" and "declaring" to their activities. When Paul stood before those in authority, he was "explaining "the kingdom of God (Acts 28).

Kingdom leadership is an interactive relationship with the King, leading to a way of life that seeks the rule of God by participating with God in his activity in the world. Its measurement is seeking, proclaiming, and waiting rather than building. When someone in authority proclaims that their leadership attitudes and activities are building or advancing the kingdom, beware. There is a good chance they do not understand kingdom leadership. They may be simply employing marketplace leadership principles in kingdom work.

Frequency #2. Kingdom leaders influence rather than control. The natural, normal way of leadership is concerned about control, command, and conquest. These three elements of leadership are experienced day in and day out by all of us. Empires are built and maintained with control. However, the model of the king is one of influence and incarnation. Simply stated, influence allows a person to make a decision. Incarnation is the experience of the one in authority coming alongside and serving together in the activity of God. A demand often is still made, but the recipient has a choice in his or her response. The incarnational presence of the King dispenses any sense of control or command. A holy partnership is experienced when kingdom leadership is practiced.

A great example of influence is the story of the carrot, the egg, and the coffee bean.[40] Influence is like a pot of boiling water. Place an egg into boiling water and in minutes it becomes hard and edible. Place a carrot into the pot and in minutes it becomes soft and edible. Place coffee beans into the pot and shortly you have a cup of coffee. With each food item, the water influenced the outcome of the experience of boiling water. The response of each item was inherent in what it was. Each item had usefulness once it was influenced. When we influence people toward the purposes of God, the outcomes of our influence are determined by the Lord. As the apostle Paul says in 1 Corinthians 3:6–9,

> I planted the seed, Apollos watered it, but God has been making it grow. So neither the one who plants nor the one who waters is anything, but only God, who makes things grow. The one who plants and the one who waters have one purpose, and they will each be rewarded according to their own labor. For we are co-workers in God's service; you are God's field, God's building.

The Lord does the building, we employ human influence, and the outcomes are determined by the Lord.

CHAPTER THIRTEEN

Frequency #3. Kingdom leaders work from inside out rather than outside in. Transformation is at the heart of kingdom leadership. Transformation occurs in the one leading, the group associated with the one leading, and those impacted by the group. The intended outcome of kingdom leadership is to experience and witness transformation.

The Lord always begins with the heart. When he was disappointed with the leadership of his people, God made a change because he wanted a "man after his own heart" to lead his people (1 Samuel 13:14). When communicating the selection of a new leader, God told the prophet Samuel, "Do not consider his appearance or his height, for I have rejected him. The LORD does not look at the things people look at. People look at the outward appearance, but the LORD looks at the heart" (1 Samuel 16:7).

Throughout Scripture, God has a history of moving the hearts of leaders. He "hardened the heart of Pharaoh" when his people left Egypt (Exodus 14:8), and he made the Egyptians "favorably disposed toward the people" when they left (12:36). "The LORD moved the heart of Cyrus king of Persia" when it was time for them to return to their homeland (2 Chronicles 36:22). He moved people to build the temple when they returned to the land (Ezra 1:5), and he placed in Nehemiah's heart the strategy to resettle the city after the wall had been rebuilt (Nehemiah 7:5). The proverb is true: "The king's heart is like a stream of water directed by the LORD; he guides it wherever he pleases" (Proverbs 21:1 NLT). He promises to give his people "a heart to know" him (Jeremiah 24:7), and to "remove from you your heart of stone and give you a heart of flesh" (Ezekiel 36:26). When his purposes are being carried out, he begins with the heart.

When Jesus reprimanded the people concerning how they were living, he also focused on the heart. "For the mouth speaks what the heart is full of. The good man brings good things out of the good stored up in him, and the evil man brings evil things out of the evil stored up in him" (Matthew 12:34–35). According to Jesus, the heart is the source of the actions of man (Mark 7:14–23). Kingdom leadership focuses on the internal, enabling lasting transformation. Attitudes and actions change as hearts change.

The temptation for leadership, when desiring to make changes, is to begin by demanding certain actions of followers. Goals are set, priorities are established, controls are put in place, and policies are made to effect change. Bold statements are communicated, and prayers are offered asking the Lord to bless and help. All this is good and at times needed. But this is not the place to start. Kingdom leadership begins with the heart. It influences people toward the purposes of God by starting on the inside and working out. Kingdom leaders focus on the values, motives, thoughts, and affections of those in their care. As they tend to these things, the externals begin to change as the internals are shaped and molded by God. Kingdom leaders depend on the Lord to shape the hearts of the followers and listen carefully to the Lord's directions concerning the actions that need to be taken.

In my observations of life, there is one entity, the military, that has the ability to bring about change from the outside in. They will take anyone and with external measures and disciplined training, tear a person down to the point where he or she is completely broken and then build that person and others together as a unit to go into the field as a bonded team to accomplish the mission. All other entities on earth fail when they attempt transformation from an external source.

Someone has said, "If an egg is broken by an outside force, life ends. If broken by an inside force, life begins. Great things always begin from the inside."[41] This is the design of God.

Seeking rather than building, influencing rather than controlling, and changing from the inside out rather than outside in are the frequencies by which we measure kingdom leadership.

KINGDOM TAKEAWAY

How do you distinguish the difference between marketplace leadership and leadership in the kingdom? What characteristics identify leadership that brings honor and delight to the Lord?

CHAPTER FOURTEEN
SOUND WAVES

Now when David had served God's purpose in his own generation, he fell asleep; he was buried with his ancestors and his body decayed.
Acts 13:36

Do your best to present yourself to God as one approved, a worker who does not need to be ashamed and who correctly handles the word of truth.
2 Timothy 2:15

The first step to grow is to gain knowledge about yourself, your people, your industry, and the principles of leadership.
Ken Blanchard, Great Leaders Grow

You see things and you say, "WHY?" But I dream things that never were; and I say: "Why not"
George Bernard Shaw, Back to Methuseleh

A sound wave is a "pattern of disturbance caused by the movement of energy traveling through a medium (such as air, water or any other liquid or solid matter) as it propagates away from the source of the sound."[42] Simply put, a sound wave is movement.

Leaders are doers. They challenge the status quo, creating a new and preferred future. They create disruption that leads to a new way. They are not satisfied with things as they are and work to make them what they should or could be. Leaders make waves.

When a person desires to provide leadership service as an influencer in the kingdom, wave-making comes from an internal motivation, a sense of destiny, to see the world as God intended it to be. Hearing God's call, responding by living a God-arranged life, and understanding all that transpires in your life as from the good hand of God preparing and shaping you in a holy partnership, creates a sense of destiny in exerting influence toward the purposes of God.

For the first eleven years of my life, my grandmother lived with us. We had a very special relationship. When I was nine, at what we called "revival meetings," the speaker talked about sin. During the day I had mistreated my brother and was still feeling guilty about it. When the speaker asked anyone who wanted to receive forgiveness to come forward, I responded. In childlike fashion but with deep sincerity, I prayed to receive forgiveness for my sin. "Asking Jesus into my heart" was the terminology used to describe my prayer. Grandma had not attended that evening, so when we got home, I rushed into her room, woke her up from sleeping, and excitedly told her. "Grandma, Grandma, I asked Jesus into my heart." Grandma, a heavyset German lady, sat up on the side of the bed, made me kneel in front of her, took a doily from her nightstand, and placed it on her head. (Grandma never prayed without a head covering). Then she laid her hands on my head and prayed a prayer of blessing. I do not remember what she prayed, but to this day I am convinced her prayer set the tone for my life that is still being answered today. From my perspective, my destiny as a person and a leader was set at that moment in time.

CHAPTER FOURTEEN

I confess I do not fully understand the call of God on the life of a leader. I only know it happens and can be confirmed later when looking back. Jeremiah was "set apart" before he was born (Jeremiah 1:5). Samuel was a little boy when he heard the voice of the Lord call him by name, "Samuel! Samuel!" (1 Samuel 3). David was a young man taking care of sheep when the prophet Samuel paid a visit to the family and "took the horn of oil and anointed him (16:13). Moses was established in a vocation when he heard God calling him "from within the bush" that was burning with a non-consuming fire (Exodus 3:4). Isaiah was up in age and worshipping the Lord when he experienced a vision, calling him to "go and tell this people" (Isaiah 6:9). Simon, Andrew, James, and John were going about their work as fishermen when Jesus invited, "Come, follow me" (Matthew 4:19). Matthew was practicing his trade of collecting taxes by the side of the road when Jesus said, "Follow me" (Matthew 9:9). Saul was on a mission to destroy those who were followers of Jesus when "a light from heaven flashed around him" (Acts 9:3) and a voice from heaven called him. From that point on, the man we know as Paul proclaimed the name of Jesus to primarily non-Jewish people, including kings. The pages of Scripture are full of people experiencing the call of God on their lives, resulting in a clear mission and destiny fulfilling the mission of God on earth. These selected examples demonstrate the creativity of God, irrespective of age or vocation.

All of us are called to serve. Some are chosen to lead. When chosen to lead, identifying the influences that have shaped our lives, preparing us for leadership, can lead to discovering why we have been chosen to lead. One way to explore these influences is to write a case study on yourself. What follows are the categories and questions to explore, along with a personal illustration of each. I hope these encourage you as you write your own personal case study.

Personal Case Study

Background/Historical Information

Create a time line or mosaic of your life.

Depending on your personality, a linear time line or a mind map of your life can reveal significant influences that have molded you into the person and leader you are today. Commitments you made, passions you expressed, values you hold, events that took place, past accomplishments and failures, all these placed on a time line or mind map provide a bird's-eye view of your life.

Commitments to Jesus, made as a child and later as an adult; to the love of my life as a nineteen-year-old; to serve the church vocationally; to church planting and later to leadership development all have been foundational to my life and personal leadership development. Relevance and integrity surface as my primary values. Determination and resolve are evident in how I live my life.

Description of Situations and People

Who and what influenced you?

Reflect over the years on whose voice has captured your attention. Who has invested in you and been there for you when needed most? Who has spoken into your life? What situations, planned or arbitrary, have motivated you to make changes or opened up new understandings?

Over the years, the people who have influenced me are my Grandma Mendel, whose influence still touches my soul after all these years; Henry Schmidt, whose influence shaped my understanding of ministry; Mr. Sellberg, who taught me about business and economics while in college; Richard Kriegbaum, who mentored me in higher education; Leonard Sweet, whose writing and conversations shaped my thinking; Pat McLaughlin, who taught me about fundraising; and my wife, Peg.

CHAPTER FOURTEEN

> *Situations that rank high on the influence scale are saying no to going home to farm after college, singing at the Probe '72 Congress on Evangelism, failing at our first attempt to plant a church, attending seminary, and pursuing a doctorate. These had significant impact on who I have become.*

Revealing Moments

What decisions have you made that reveal who you are?

Major decisions often reveal something about us. Make a list of decisions you made that were big. A career or job change. Moving to a new location. A relationship decision. Stop and reflect on those major decisions. What do they reveal about you?

In 1982 we packed all we had into a Ryder truck and a Zephyr station wagon and moved with our three preschool children to Houston, Texas, to start churches with our supporting denomination. After two and a half years of ministry, we could count over five hundred people whose lives we had impacted, but there was no organized church to show for the ministry. The supporting denomination decided to pull out, and we were left without support. They expected us to relocate and assume a pastorate at another church. However, we had no peace about leaving Houston. As best we understood it, we had been called by God to Houston to start a church. Moving from Houston would mean either that initially, we had not heard correctly from the Lord, or that he wanted us to remain until a church was started. We chose the latter interpretation. I became a bi-vocational church planter. We discovered another denomination that was looking for church planters, and we remained in Houston. We continued to serve as church planters and by God's grace witnessed his raising up a church. As I reflect on the experience, it reveals the determination and resolve with which I approach life and leadership.

Defining Moments

What events and incidents shaped who you are?

Life is a series of experiences. Some of them have deep impact on us and become a defining moment when the trajectory of our lives is altered, often permanently. Sometimes we enter these events intentionally. Other times they surprise us. They can be broken-world experiences, or they can be personal best accomplishments. They happen, and we are never the same because of them. Deaths, pink slips, bad investments, illnesses, and broken relationships often are defining moments. Awards, promotions, achievements, affirmations, and honors can also serve as defining moments.

The pink slip from the denomination when they pulled out of Houston was certainly one of these experiences. My preaching was forever changed by the bi-vocational church-planting experience. Attending seminary and pursuing doctoral work could be listed as life changing. But the most significant life-altering moment was when my alma mater invited me to serve as their president. It had never been on my radar, but suddenly I was asked to lead an educational institution that I loved, but I had no clue what was involved.

Root Cause Analysis

What causes you to act the way you do?

Problem-solving in industry by doing a root cause analysis is a way to discover the real reason for something that has not gone as planned. Like peeling an artichoke, a root cause analysis gets to the heart of the problem, allowing you to address a tipping-point need. Apply this to your life when you look at your leadership actions. What motivates you to take the action you do? Why do you choose the people you do to report directly to you? Why do you implement the strategies or pursue the action plans you undertake? What continually motivates you to do what you naturally do?

CHAPTER FOURTEEN

> Demanding productivity and practicing compassion are two characteristics of my leadership activity. I am aware that these both come from a root cause of anger in my life that I dealt with during my seminary days. I grew up in a setting where anger was a way of life. Processing and understanding anger and its destructive ways helped me develop a heart of compassion. The same would be true with the drive to succeed.

Central Issues Faced

What personal issue is always present in your life?

Everyone has a story. Behind every reaction is a story. When interfacing with people in life, their attitudes and actions have a story influencing them. In many cases, there is a central issue that continues to raise its head repeatedly.

My daughter's response to me when I was telling the family how much I enjoyed serving as president of the college describes best my central issue: "Dad, just admit it: you like being in charge." I had been discovered. She was right. Although being in charge has its advantages, there are many disadvantages when it becomes a driver in your life.

Description of Leadership Situations

Where and how did you practice leadership?

Another time line or mosaic might be helpful. List all the times when you were asked to provide leadership. What was your first leadership experience? What was your most significant leadership experience? List every situation where you provided leadership, formally or informally. As you reflect on each, summarize, in a sentence of two, the experience. Was it a good or bad experience? What did you learn from it? What were the circumstances surrounding the experience? Usually there are some surprises with this one.

When I made the list, I discovered that my entire life, from my high school church youth group to the college presidency, I gravitated toward leadership assignments with most groups I engaged in. The assignments that captured my imagination most were launching a camping ministry for the denomination while pastoring, serving as dean of a seminary, and being a college president. These three became my personal best leadership experiences. In each of these, God smiled down in rewarding and fulfilling ways.

Analysis and Evaluation of Yourself

Summarize what you see and who you are.

Now take a deep breath, read Psalm 139, ask the Lord to open your eyes and heart, and begin to assess all you have written. Reread Psalm 139. As with a kaleidoscope, turn the tube, looking at all the designs, and marvel at what God has done in and through you. Then settle on one of the designs that captures your imagination most. You have been called to serve. You have been chosen to lead. Celebrate the call of God.

I felt liberated when I discovered I was a visionary leader with a creative, action-oriented style that engages people and is very pragmatic. This discovery taught me what kind of people I needed around me to be effective and where my blind spots were as a leader. When criticism came, I was able to accept it knowing it was probably accurate.

Possible Destiny

Why did God place you on this earth?

I wish I could say that once you have gone through the reflection process outlined in this chapter, you will know without a doubt your destiny. At best you will be able to craft a personal mission statement and move forward with a confidence that only comes from the Lord. At

CHAPTER FOURTEEN

> worst you will humbly stand before the Lord, continuing to seek him and his ways for your life.
>
> My experience affirmed my personal mission statement of "to honor and trust God with my life by being a person of influence, inspiring and impacting with relevance and integrity the lives of those who will influence others."
>
> In my retirement, I am living in the afterglow of a life of service. I no longer seek opportunities to serve and lead. I wait for them to come and respond as I sense God's voice calling me to serve. The waves I now create are small. The situations around me are mostly calm. I know the day will come when I will meet the One who called me and whom I have desired to serve with relevance and integrity. When I see his face, I will fall on my face before him with a grateful heart. I only hope I will hear him say, "Well done, my good and faithful servant. Enter into my presence, where all is well and there is no time."

As you engage in examining your life and leadership, seeking to understand the call of God on your life, remember that you are not who you think you are or who people say you are. You are who God says you are. According to Ephesians 2:10, you are "…God's masterpiece. He has created us anew in Christ Jesus, so we can do the good things he planned for us long ago." (NLT)

> **KINGDOM TAKEAWAY**
>
> Reflect on God's call on your life and leadership. Using the questions in this chapter, take time to create a case study of yourself. What do you learn about yourself?

CHAPTER FIFTEEN
SOUND EFFECTS

But what happens when we live God's way? He brings gifts into our lives, much the same way that fruit appears in an orchard—things like affection for others, exuberance about life, serenity. We develop a willingness to stick with things, a sense of compassion in the heart, and a conviction that a basic holiness permeates things and people. We find ourselves involved in loyal commitments, not needing to force our way in life, able to marshal and direct our energies wisely.
Galatians 5:22–23 *(The Message)*

People don't leave bad jobs; they leave because of bad leaders, poor management and a lack of appreciation for their worth.
Leadership First

Culture creates behaviors. Behaviors reinforce culture.
Attributed to Andy Stanley

I remember listening as a little boy at four o'clock on Saturday afternoons to *Unshackled*, the radio program of Pacific Garden Mission in Chicago. Each week featured a story of a person who had experienced a life change resulting from the ministry of the mission.

CHAPTER FIFTEEN

To highlight the dramatic vocal presentation of the story, an organist would interject sound effects. These sound effects were like punctuation marks in the oral storytelling. Often, they created suspense. What would happen next? Some sixty years later I can still, with my imagination, hear the sound effects of that radio program.

A sound effect is a noise created to enhance and emphasize a performance or experience. From movies to video games, television shows to commercials, dramatic productions to concerts, car enthusiasts to athletic competitions, sound effects are used to engage the participants, drawing them into the experience and eliciting a response. Compare an athletic competition with and without a band. Sound effects are about presentation of the event. The sound effect can be pleasant or unpleasant, loud or soft, dissonant or harmonious, depending on the response you want from the listener.

When the Lord was initiating a community of people who would know him and experience his deliverance and providing a land for them to make their home, he came down to Mount Sinai to speak to the people. As a demonstration of his holiness and all-consuming power, he used sound effects to place the "fear of God" into the people: "On the morning of the third day there was thunder and lightning, with a thick cloud over the mountain, and a very loud trumpet blast. Everyone in the camp trembled" (Exodus 19:16). The Lord came down from the heavens, and his escorts were thunder and a loud trumpet.

At my inauguration as president of Tabor College, the Symphonic Band played Concerto in B-Flat for Two Trumpets as the academic processional entered the gymnasium for the service. We could have walked in silence and taken our seats. Instead, everything was choreographed as the board chair led the way, introducing us to the audience to a majestic sound, signaling the audience to stand at the exact time I entered the room, and creating a moment of awe and adoration. I confess, I felt both humbled and honored at the same time. My ego was massaged, yet I felt so unworthy.

Each year at commencement I led the academic procession while the band played "Pomp and Circumstance." The faculty, administration, and graduating students could have just walked in, yelling and screaming, but we chose to add sound effects as we marched, bringing a sentimental response to the participants.

Leaders create effects. Their attitudes and actions elicit a response from those engaged in the mission. Their presence can inspire or dishearten the people. Corporate cultures are created by the effects of leadership. Confidence, excitement, and discipline can all be high due to the voice, tone, and mood of the person in charge. Or there can be apathy, discouragement, and fear due to the ways and means of the leader.

I have observed over the years that positive, healthy, and thriving cultures are created when the person called to influence has an attitude of gratitude, humility, generosity, and transparency and together with the people, takes responsibility, recognizes that decisions have consequences, and learns from failure. These attitudes and practices have a life-giving effect on the people.

When serving as dean of a seminary, I was charged with making it a financially viable and sustainable school for the university. One month into my tenure, a senior administrator informed me that consideration was being given to close the school due to the financial strain. I asked for at least a year to plant some seeds that could possibly produce a harvest for the university. She agreed.

One year later, by the grace of God and with the influence of Dr. Leonard Sweet, a unique doctoral program was launched that was both profitable and highly influential in training men and women to provide kingdom-seeking, culturally relevant, and biblically rooted leadership. The faculty bought into the idea and were motivated to creatively engage in further program development that expanded the influence of the seminary. An entrepreneurial spirit began to take hold. We celebrated improvement and advancement. Incentives were granted, and affirmations were given in abundance. This high-capacity and extremely brilliant faculty turned the seminary into a viable and sustainable school. I am told that donkeys are often placed in the same field with horses to create a calming effect on the horses. I often felt like a donkey with a bunch of racehorses. The entire team worked diligently, and together, with the affirmation of the Lord, we began to break even and then contribute to the financial bottom line of the university. The culture of the seminary changed, and the results were affirmed. Gratitude, humility, generosity, and transparency were evident in all aspects of the school.

All of us have a bent toward that which is not good. We so easily miss the mark set for us by the Master Leader, giving in to temptations to think more highly of ourselves, always wanting more, and misleading and being dishonest with others. Pride, greed, and deceit have derailed many a leader who proclaims to honor and trust God in leadership. The effect of these attitudes on the groups they are leading are a loss of confidence, apathy, and reduced engagement. Each of us knows someone whose arrogance, greediness, and dishonesty brought about heartache and disappointment.

As I have heard it said, "you can afford to be right and stubborn." You can afford to be wrong and humble. You cannot afford to be wrong and stubborn. When pride, greed, and deceit are evident in a leader's life, the effect is one of eventual disaster. However, when gratitude is shown, humility is demonstrated, generosity is practiced, and transparency is displayed, people respond with determination, engagement, and productivity. These attitudes bring out the best in people by motivating them to give their best.

We live in a BCD (blame, complain, and defend) culture. It is always someone else's fault. The situation is bad. I am a victim. I have my rights. We observe this in political leaders, marketplace leaders, institutional leaders, nonprofit leaders, and church leaders. Repeatedly, things will not go as planned or desired. The larger the workforce under your care, the greater the possibility of things not going well. When negative things happen, the natural response is to blame someone, complain about the situation, and defend our actions. The effect is demoralizing and discouraging, making for an unhealthy and toxic environment.

Rather than blaming someone, take responsibility. Own your actions and decisions. Recognize that somewhere along the line, you made a decision that is now bearing the fruit of the seed you sowed with that decision. All decisions have consequences. Depending on your area of service, the lag time from when making the decision to experiencing the consequences can vary. In higher education there is an eighteen- to twenty-four-month period until you see the fruit of your decisions. In some cases, it can happen within weeks or months. The seeds of the harvest you are experiencing now were sown sometime in the past. When the consequences are not what you desired, take responsibility, learn from the failure, and make the needed adjustments. Improvement cannot materialize unless you take responsibility, recognize your decisions have consequences, and learn from failures.

We were driving in the car with two of our grandchildren when something was said about someone losing a job. One of the grandchildren asked me, "Gramps, have you ever fired someone?"

"Yes, I have," I replied.

"Why did you fire them?" she asked.

"Because they did not take responsibility."

Sensing this was a teachable moment, I told my grandchildren about a specific time when I had relieved someone of his duties.

"One time," I began, "a team of two people made some bad decisions, and the consequences were very bad for us. Lots of people were hurt by their decisions and actions, and this reflected badly on the organization. I called them both in and asked them to explain to me what had happened. The first person immediately said, 'Dr. Glanzer, I take responsibility for this. I made a mistake and did not do what I should have done. I am sorry. If you want me to resign, I will.'

CHAPTER FIFTEEN

"The second person had a completely different attitude and response," I continued. "He blamed others, complained about why it had happened, assured me he had not done anything wrong, and repeatedly stated that he had done what was required. His entire response was blame, complain, and defend.

"I fired the second person because he did not take responsibility," I concluded.

By the way, the first person in that story, not only did I continue to employ him, but I promoted him shortly after that, because he learned from his failure. We can only learn from our failures when we take responsibility for our actions. Blaming, complaining, and defending lead to a toxic culture. Their effect demotivates, demoralizes, and destroys engagement, meaningfulness, and happiness in the workplace.

When we are chosen to lead, our attitudes and practices have effects on those in our care. And if we do not keep them in check, we and the organizations we lead are adversely affected.

Words of wisdom from Proverbs 4 seem appropriate: "Above all else, guard your heart, for everything you do flows from it" (v. 23).

And how does that happen? By watching how you talk, where you focus, the direction you take, and dealing with evil. As Proverbs continues,

> Keep your mouth free of perversity; keep corrupt talk far from your lips.
>
> Let your eyes look straight ahead; fix your gaze directly before you.
>
> Give careful thought to the paths for your feet and be steadfast in all your ways.
>
> Do not turn to the right or the left; keep your foot from evil.
> (Proverbs 4:24-27)

KINGDOM TAKEAWAY

Where in your life and leadership do you need to take responsibility? What seeds have you sown and what kind of harvest are you reaping?

CHAPTER SIXTEEN
SOUND OF SILENCE

*"Be still, and know that I am God;
I will be exalted among the nations,
I will be exalted in the earth."*
Psalm 46:10

Set your minds on things above, not on earthly things.
Colossians 3:2

In repentance and rest is your salvation, in quietness and trust is your strength, but you would have none of it.
Isaiah 30:15

Search me, God, and know my heart; test me and know my anxious thoughts. See if there is any offensive way in me and lead me in the way everlasting.
Psalm 139:23–24

Ruthlessly eliminate hurry from your life.
Attributed to Dallas Willard

Leaders who want to honor God with their influence are continually asking, "What does God want me to do?" Mission, vision, values,

CHAPTER SIXTEEN

strategies, actions, and decisions of all kinds are brought before the Lord for his guidance. Providing kingdom-seeking, God-honoring, biblically rooted influence requires that one has an ongoing, intimate interaction with God. "God's guidance is but one dimension of a richly interactive relationship."[43] The sound of this guidance can come through daily living, practicing spiritual disciplines, and silence.

I had four credit hours of coursework left to complete my doctoral work in leadership and church management. After reading thousands of pages on leadership, and writing almost as many, there was still something missing in my study of leadership. I identified the missing link as the spiritual dimension of leadership. I asked and received permission to engage in an independent study on leadership and spiritual formation with Dr. Dallas Willard as my professor. He graciously agreed. I met with him and began my private study of the topic.

After 120 credits of undergraduate work, 96 credits of master's-level work, and 32 doctoral-level credits, the four hours of credit as independent study in leadership and spiritual formation with Dr. Willard were the most impactful of all my educational credits. One of the assignments was a twenty-four-hour solitude and silence retreat. Dr. Willard's instructions were simple: I was to go to a place where there was no one else and no noise of any kind. Then, for at least twenty-four hours, I was to do nothing. Be unproductive. I could only walk, observe, read scripture, and ask God to speak. I was to take only my Bible, and a hymnbook if I wanted, but stay out of study mode. Do not fast, he advised, but rather eat lightly. Mary's Song and the Psalms were suggested for meditation. I could write my thoughts, but that was not essential or even recommended. I was to write about the experience a couple of weeks later, not right away.

The night before I began the experience, I called Dr. Willard. After a short chat telling him my plan, he closed the conversation with, "Have a wonderful meeting with the Lord. Let God come to you. It will be an experience of grace."

God came to me during the experience in a profound way. Sometime later I wrote in my journal, "My life is mastered by a desire to produce. I want to constantly be making something or accomplishing something. When I'm alone, I'm dreaming or thinking about a problem or situation. I want to produce. Why?"

The solitude and silence retreat became a regular discipline of mine. Something broke inside me that first time and altered my understanding and practice of leadership. I discovered being is as important if not more important than doing. Pride, greed, and deceit are always knocking on the door, asking to do their thing. The answer is not managing them but confessing them. Noise, hurry, and the voice of the crowd easily keep me from leading from a divine center. The regular practice of solitude and silence help overcome these obstacles. My walk with God had become so production oriented that I had forgotten how to just be with God. Behold him. Enjoy him. Hear him. I learned to interact with him as the living Word and experience his revelation through nature and what he is doing in the world.

Practicing the disciplines of solitude and silence clears the decks to receive guidance from the Lord. Each time the experience is different. Rest, inner peace, missional guidance, getting off the treadmill of life, and attitude adjustments are some of the experiences I had during these times of aloneness. The conversation is interesting when it is just me, myself, and I plus God. Sometimes I do not like being with the first three. But God still shows up. Sometimes he speaks. Sometimes he's silent. And sometimes he just holds me. But he always comes in grace.

As part of the Presidential Leadership Scholars program, I took the group on a solitude and silence experience. The first time the students were very nervous. Giving up their phones, eating in silence, and being alone all day raised their anxiety level beyond description. However, after that first year, word got out among the students, and each group after that would ask when we were going to go on the solitude and silence retreat. It became one of the highlights of the program.

When we hear the phrase "Sound of Silence," my generation thinks of Simon and Garfunkel singing their popular song by that name. When Paul Simon was asked about the meaning of the song, he said it was a song about "the inability of people to communicate with each other, not particularly intentionally, but especially emotionally, so what you see around you are people unable to love each other."[44] Our relationship with the master influencer can be described in a similar way. Our inability to communicate with the

CHAPTER SIXTEEN

Lord, although not intentional, but emotionally can keep us from loving God with all our hearts, soul, mind, and strength.

The sound of silence can change that. The sound of silence is not Simon and Garfunkel singing their song. The sound of silence is the Lord providing guidance to those he has called to fulfill his mission on earth.

When I assumed the presidency of a college, I contacted Dr. Willard and asked him what advice he would give me. "Ruthlessly eliminate hurry from your life," he responded. Engaging in a solitude and silence experience and practicing guided prayer are ways to eliminate hurry, noise, and the voice of the crowd.

I confess I was not able to follow his advice to the degree I should have, but I did learn the importance of solitude and silence when providing leadership. Beginning most days in solitude and silence beholding, enjoying, and listening to him was an essential discipline in fulfilling God's call on my life influencing those in my care to fulfill the purposes of God on earth.

If you desire to engage in a solitude and silence experience, a helpful guide is provided in Appendix A.

> **KINGDOM TAKEAWAY**
> Using the Guided Prayer in Appendix B, spend 100 minutes (10 minutes for each phase) in prayer."

POSTLUDE
CREATING A MAGNUM OPUS

*Since my youth, God, you have taught me,
and to this day I declare your marvelous deeds.
Even when I am old and gray,
do not forsake me, my God,
till I declare your power to the next generation,
your mighty acts to all who are to come.*
Psalm 71:17–18

The growth and development of people is the highest calling of leadership.
Attributed to Harvey Firestone

Leaders don't create followers. They create more leaders.
Tom Peters, in "Rule #3," *Fast Company*

A "magnum opus" is one's greatest piece of work. Most agree that Leonardo da Vinci's magnum opus is the Mona Lisa. The Old Man and the Sea is considered Ernest Hemingway's greatest work. Likewise, Johann Sebastian Bach's Mass in B Minor is often listed as his magnum opus. Critics do not agree whether the movie E.T. or Schindler's List is producer Steven Spielberg's greatest work.

Each of us can have a magnum opus. Architects, engineers, CEO, teachers, contractors, professors, medical researchers—what-

POSTLUDE

ever your vocation, you can have a magnum opus. If you are a cook, it could be your hand-made chicken cordon bleu that everyone raves over and likes. Or if you are a landscaper, the beautiful botanical garden you create can be your magnum opus. Although the term most often refers to literature, music, and artwork, it can describe any great work of a person.

In the movie *Mr. Holland's Opus*, a high school music teacher, Glenn Holland, who always wanted to be a composer and write a musical magnum opus, discovered that his real magnum opus was his students, their lives, and the influence he had on them over the years. Mr. Holland lived his legacy his entire life and in the end discovered his true magnum opus.

Another example is Dr. Nachtigall, an orthopedic surgeon. When I visited his office, I noticed the hallway was full of 8" × 10" professional pictures of various men and women. When I asked who they were, he said they were surgeons whom over the years he had taught how to perform his specialty of back surgery. I did not count the pictures, but his goal before he retired was to train one hundred orthopedic surgeons. He reached the goal and upon his retirement was given a bronze tree signifying the many surgeons he trained. Significant to the training was the mission work they did, which those he trained now continue to do in their respective practices. Of all the work this well-loved doctor had performed over the years, the training of these surgeons and their subsequent commitment to mission work as part of their respective practices was his pride and joy. He had lived his legacy, and they were his magnum opus.

The magnum opus of a leader could be a significant project he or she oversees, an ingenious strategy he or she implements, or a major desired change he or she effects. Any personal best can receive the label "magnum opus." But I would contend that a leader's real magnum opus is the leaders he or she equips and inspires to influence others. The best leaders create more leaders. Effective leaders are more concerned about creating more leaders than completing a project or enlarging the groups they are leading. The leaders they create together become a symphonic legacy of influence. This is the ultimate sound of leadership: one generation of leaders investing in the lives of the next generation to create a sweet melody to the Voice of One, who is looking for those who will influence toward his purpose on earth.

While I was in seminary, Dr. Henry Schmidt brought together three students who met early each Friday morning for bad coffee, donuts, and discussion about *The Measure of a Man* by Gene Getz. Throughout my lifetime, Henry continued to pour into me, investing in my life and leadership thinking. When I went to his funeral, I discovered dozens of people like me in whom Henry had invested over the years. We were his magnum opus. His influence in my life shaped my personal vision and mission statement and facilitated a reconciliation with my father.

When I told my father I was not coming home to continue the family farm after college, his lifelong dream was shattered. For about two years, our relationship was strained. While at seminary, Henry Schmidt paid him a visit. Henry brought back a box of candy with a three-by-five-inch notecard written by Dad. I still have this card in the flyleaf of my Bible. The words of 2 Timothy 2:1–2, referenced in the note, are still the focus of my leadership: "You then, my son, be strong in the grace that is in Christ Jesus. And the things you have heard me say in the presence of many witnesses entrust to reliable people who will also be qualified to teach others."

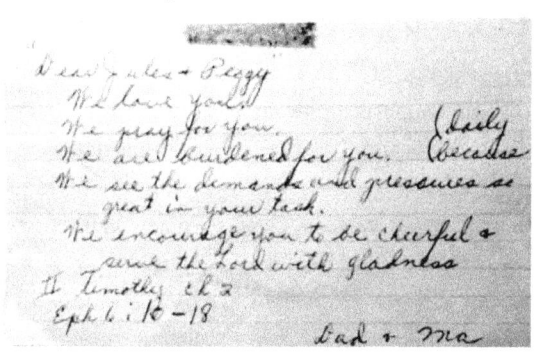

Earlier I shared my personal mission statement, "to honor and trust God with my life by being a person of influence, impacting and inspiring with relevance and integrity, the lives of those who will influence others." In retirement I added "one person at a time." When I originally wrote the statement, I also expanded on what it meant to me. I wanted at the end of my life to be able to make a list of leaders I have been instrumental in developing. My magnum opus has, is, and will be individuals whom I have influenced to be leaders in their own right. No title or position is needed. Just give your life to influencing others toward the purposes of God on earth. Infuse the vision and values of the eternal into the temporal while at the same time storing up treasures on the other side with the service and influence you have on this side.

For all leaders, like Henry Schmidt, Mr. Holland, and the many others that are known for their effective influence, a leader's magnum opus is creating other leaders who together create the sound of leadership.

Creating a magnum opus of more leaders is an experience that begins with ideas, requires reflection, involves participation, needs relationship, and is best expressed in entrepreneurship and service.

I was nervous when I stood up in front of the faculty and staff of the college that I was leading at our annual All Employee Spring Luncheon. I stated that we were not in the business of providing an education but rather of providing an experience for our students. No degree of influence, debate, or evidence could persuade most of the people in the room that my statement was true. After all, we were a college, a place committed to Christian higher education. Our task was to inspire students to think critically, discover truth, and embrace a life of Christian vocation. Those gathered that day were convinced that the experience was secondary to our mission. Providing examples from *Harvard Business Review*'s classic article "Marketing Myopia"[45] did little to sway the thinking in the room. Yet, it is a conviction of mine that all colleges provide an experience unique to them that shapes the lives of their students. It is totally appropriate for a prospective student to ask, "What kind of person will I become if I attend this college?" The content, textbooks, and journal articles are basically the same throughout higher education curricula. But the experience of the respective colleges is what makes them unique. Despite not convincing the audience that day, I still maintain that attending college and leadership development is an experience.

The leadership development experience **begins with ideas**. We live at the mercy of our ideas. Before one has a feeling, takes an action, or speaks a word, there is an idea. I have stood by a casket with no emotion. What was I thinking? *I do not know who this is.* I have also stood by a casket and broken down and wept uncontrollably. What was I thinking? *Mom, I need you.* What I thought determined my emotion. Same with developing as a leader. The ideas around discovering who I am, pursuing a vision, establishing a strategic direction, or making a difficult decision all begin with an idea, a thought, a value, or a philosophy. Increasing one's capacity as a leader begins with assessing a person and his or her activity as a leader. As A. R. Bernard said, "The quality of your thoughts determines the quality of your life."[46]

The leadership development experience **requires reflection**. Ideas need processing. Someone has said that the longest eighteen inches in the world are those between the head and the heart. For ideas to take root in the heart, reflection is required. Solitude and silence, assessment and evaluation, and integration and application are needed as the ideas we are exposed to are made a part of our life and leadership. Intentionally removing ourselves from the clutter and noise of life and spending time alone with God and "me, myself, and I" is essential to having those ideas take root in our hearts. Not all ideas are helpful. Processing them through the filter of scripture, listening to the Voice of One, and giving oneself to prayerfully considering the truth behind the ideas are important in our development as leaders.

The leadership development experience **involves participation**. Leaders are doers. The famed artist Pablo Picasso also understood this. He is attributed with saying, "Action is the foundational key to all success."[47] So often we wait for perfect timing or perfect plans while mustering the courage to take action. General Patton's wisdom is worthy to be considered by any leader: "A good plan violently executed *now* is better than a perfect plan next week."[48] To grow in your leadership capacity, take the risk, muster the courage, and engage in activity that has the potential to move you and your group toward the intended outcome and the preferred future. Experience comes from taking risks, practicing courage, and engaging in activity. Walt Disney said it best: the way to get started is to quit talking and begin doing.[49] As a motivation for me to take action, I have on my desk, etched in glass, the Possibility Thinker's Creed written by Dr. Robert Schuller. "When faced with a mountain, I will not quit! I will keep on striving until I climb over, find a pass through, tunnel underneath, or simply stay and turn the mountain into a gold mine—with God's help!"[50] We are in a partnership with the Lord himself as we engage with him in his activity in the world to fulfill his mission. As stated in Psalm 127:1: "Unless the LORD builds the house, the builders labor in vain. Unless the LORD watches over the city, the guards stand watch in vain." We are not alone in our participation.

The leadership development experience **needs relationship**. Colin Powell's understanding of leadership expands this need: "Leadership is all about people. It is not about organizations. It is not about plans. It is not about strategies. It is all about people motivating people to get the job done. You have to be people centered."[51] Essential for any person to provide leadership service is a situation that needs addressing, a group of people who desire a change for the common good, and someone who is called by God to show the way. The glue that binds these three essentials together is relationships. Relationships that are genuine, real, authentic, and can bear the weight of truth are pivotal for any leader. Proverbs 27:17 says, "As iron sharpens iron, so one person sharpens another." Increasing the capacity to lead requires the involvement of peers who will with love and transparency provide feedback and insights making you a more effective leader. We need one another to grow and increase our influence capacity.

The leadership development experience is best **expressed in service and entrepreneurship**. In the end, what is visible to the people we are called to lead is our service mentality and entrepreneurial spirit.

Getting our hands and feet dirty while practicing creativity and innovation are the metaphors people see and embrace. Having a can-do attitude and responding to new ideas with "Why not?" motivates people to follow. Every leader should have a tycoon mentality: "I create. I take risks. I live my passion. I am an entrepreneur."[52]

> **KINGDOM TAKEAWAY**
> Who are the people you have equipped and inspired to influence others? Who would have you on their list as someone who has significantly influenced their life and leadership?

POSTLUDE

Why study leadership?
Because leadership development
is a learning experience.
Leaders are learners.

So, don't study because you need to. Study . . .

because knowledge is power
because no one can take your knowledge away from you
because you want to know more
because it enhances you
because it grows you

When you study leadership . . .

you are increasing your capacity to influence
    investing in the lives of others
    providing opportunities for others to succeed
    equipping people to accomplish significant things
    inspiring people to go to new places

you are expanding your opportunity to do good
    making the world a better place
    bringing together people for the common good
    accomplishing a mission that enhances lives
    seeing a vision become reality

you are becoming who you were created to be
    understanding yourself
    understanding others
    improving your character
    expanding your leadership skills

Because everything revolves around leadership.
Leadership matters.

REPRISE
SOVEREIGN LEADERSHIP LESSONS FROM COVID-19

"For my thoughts are not your thoughts, neither are your ways my ways," declares the LORD.
"As the heavens are higher than the earth, so are my ways higher than your ways and my thoughts than your thoughts."
Isaiah 55:8–9

What was good enough yesterday may no longer be all we need today. We will build on the old so you can reposition yourself for the new era ahead.
Attributed to Jerold Panas

On November 28, 2020, my life made a major pivot. I was in day ten of having COVID-19, and my oxygen level was not holding. My personal physician said I needed supplemental oxygen. I thought I would be in the hospital for a couple of days, get some extra whiffs of O_2, and then come home.

Knowing there were year-end legal issues needing attention, I quickly wrote an email to the board chair to make arrangements for the possibility that I would not be able to fulfill my duties as president of the college. I also sent texts to family that this was a precautionary move.

When my wife dropped me off, I leaned across the console of the front seat of the car and kissed her goodbye. I checked in quickly and was taken to a normal room. Within the hour, the doctor laid out the various levels of medical therapies, and I knew this was more than a couple of whiffs of oxygen. I was hooked up to a Vapotherm unit and later a BiPAP, both of which provide noninvasive breathing support.

While on the BiPAP, I had an experience, looking back, I simply call "Vision of the Cross." I was standing in front of a very large cross, square, wooden, and brown in color, rising hundreds of feet into the air at the end of the road. It was blocking everything and there was no way around it. I sensed that behind me was my life, the world, and everything that pertained to living on earth. In front of me the cross. As I stood there, a wave of forgiveness swept over me, followed by a wave of deep confidence of salvation. No lists, no memory of sins committed, just an incredible sense of total forgiveness, deep assurance of salvation, and a peaceful serenity.

I knew this was the cross of Jesus. It was not a pretty cross. Yet, I remember thinking, *Everything in this world ends at the cross. The gate of heaven is a cross.* I sensed that if I stepped into the cross, I would be on the other side and I would see Jesus.

I reached for my phone to text Peg. "The world behind me. The cross in front of me," I wrote. "Always was and someday will be. Just do not know when." I added another text, "First, I want to see Jesus. Then if they let me, I'll wait at the gate for you and our family."

Then for a few moments I reflected. The decorative cross on my desk came into view. An affirmative thought about the direction of the college came to mind. Making and keeping the cross central to the mission of the college was deeply impressed upon me, as was living my entire life focused on the cross.

It is all about the cross, I thought. *All of life culminates at the cross. Real life begins at the cross. Lift up the cross.*

All these thoughts flooded my mind as I stood in front of the cross, contemplating the possibility of stepping into the cross and seeing Jesus. No guilt. No fear. No decision. Simply a transition from earth to heaven.

Suddenly I felt a compulsion to fight. No choice, just an inner motivation to fight. For the next four hours, with every breath I took, I fought to stay alive. My doctor later said that she has never seen someone fight so hard. The next morning, the medical staff moved me to ICU and began convalescent plasma transfusions plus remdesivir and additional steroidal drug therapies.

When they began the plasma transfusion and again as they administered the remdesivir, I prayed that as these drugs entered my bloodstream, they would wash away the virus just as Jesus' blood washed away my sin on the cross. What his blood did for me on the cross, these therapies would do to the coronavirus in my body.

A few days later, when the doctor told me the virus was no longer in my body and treatment would now focus on recovery of the lungs, it seemed as if my prayer was answered. The recovery lasted for thirty-one days in the hospital, twenty days in home health, and two years and counting.

I do not understand the sovereignty of God. I think of all those I know who lost the battle to COVID-19. Relatives, friends, colleagues, and those in the white body bags that passed my hospital room on gurneys. They too had people praying, competent medical professionals, and many drug therapies. Yet, they did not survive. I did. I now see each day as a gift from the good hand of God. I do not understand the sovereignty of God. I just know that either he is sovereign over all or he is not sovereign at all. I believe he is sovereign over all, including our leadership activities and service. Leadership lesson learned: **Leadership that is kingdom-seeking, God-honoring, and biblically rooted serves at the pleasure of the Lord**.

From my limited view, God has given me more days to serve him. The Vision of the Cross has motivated me to reset my life. It came at a perfect time as I concluded the presidency and moved into retirement. My visionary-action-oriented style of leadership was tempered for retirement. I see the hand of God in all of this. Leadership lesson learned: **His ways are beyond my capacity to understand. My responsibility is to trust him.**

I reset my life around five words impressed upon my heart during my hospital stay: *contentment, gratitude, simplicity, smallness,* and *focus.* These are the words I heard from the Voice of One. I realized Jehovah Jireh (God Our Provider) and Jehovah Rapha (God Our Healer), one God with many names, is operative in my life and leadership. I continue to listen to the Voice of One. You can too.

So listen to the invitation of the One who spoke creation into being and is still speaking today: "The Spirit and the bride say, 'Come!' And let the one who hears say, 'Come!'" (Revelation 22:17). May our ears hear God's voice and honor his call to influence his world to be all he intended it to be.

APPENDIX A

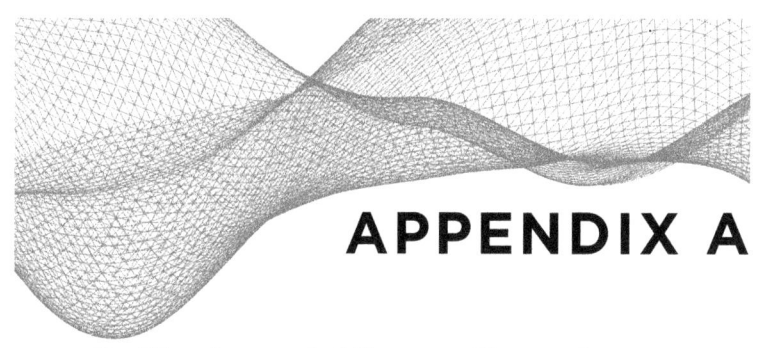

Solitude and Silence Experience

Spending time in solitude and silence can be an effective way to grow in your relationship with God. Practically, what happens is the clutter of our lives is cleared and an opportunity for God to get through arises. Each time the experience results in a different benefit. Here are some guidelines to make the time meaningful:

1. Begin with a prayer something like this: "By the authority of almighty God, I surround myself with the light of Christ, I cover myself with the blood of Christ, and I seal myself with the cross of Christ. All dark and evil spirits must now leave. No influence is allowed to come near to me but that it is first filtered through the light of Jesus Christ, in whose name I pray. Amen."[53]

2. The time frame needs to be at least a twenty-four-hour period. Remove yourself from all people, noises, and distractions. Be alone in solitude and silence. An outdoor setting is preferable.

3. Take a Bible, a pen, and a notebook. A songbook might also be helpful.

4. No devices of any kind can be brought with you.

5. Do nothing. Be unproductive. Walk, observe, listen, meditate, and ask God to speak. Be aware of what is happening in you and around you.

Appendix A

6. Read scripture. Stay out of study mode. Listen to the scripture. Meditate on the scripture. Select one passage, a short one, and stay with it the whole time (for example, Luke 1:46–55 or Psalm 23, 103, or 139).

7. Eat light. Do not fast.

8. Write your thoughts, observations, and feelings throughout the day.

9. Behold God. Wait for God. Let him come to you. It will be an experience of grace.

APPENDIX B

Guided Prayer

Find a relaxed place and spend time focusing on God by allowing his Spirit to guide you in the following phases of prayer. Build on each phase as you allow the Holy Spirit to guide you in setting your heart and mind on things above. Spend anywhere from fifteen minutes to an hour on each phase.

Phase 1: Relaxation. Slow down and be still. Unpack all the things that are on your mind. Breathe deeply and just be with God. Allow yourself to unwind and be unwound. Let God love you.

Phase 2: Awareness. Realize God is here. Think of some verses that assure you he is present. Become aware you are not alone, but God is with you right now. If it helps, imagine Jesus is sitting beside you.

Phase 3: Surrender. Give everything to God, all your dreams, disappointments, possessions, past, future, problems, family, work, and so on, all that comes to mind. Give it up to him. Surrender your will to his will. Abandon your own will. Lift it up and let it go. Release all you have and are to God. Do not ask for anything; just give.

Phase 4: Acceptance. Accept and receive God's will. Pray, "Not my will, but yours be done." Verbally accept what the God of love desires for you.

Appendix B

Phase 5: Confession, Forgiveness, and Repentance. Confess your sins. Think through the Ten Commandments and where you have broken them. Agree with God on where you have sinned. Receive his forgiveness. Allow yourself to be forgiven. Forgive others. Recall those who have hurt you and verbally forgive them for the hurtful things they have done to you.

Phase 6: Contemplation. Ask the Holy Spirit to bring to mind a story from the Bible and picture yourself in that story. Be there, on location. Imagine yourself experiencing the story. Be in touch with your senses. Hear what God has to say to you.

Phase 7: Receive the Holy Spirit. Ask to be filled with the Holy Spirit. Verbally receive the Holy Spirit.

Phase 8: Intercession. Ask God for what you need and want. Pray for your own needs. Pray for others. This is the time to make your requests of God.

Phase 9: Inquire. Seek God's guidance. Ask him to speak. What does he want you to do? Listen to him. What guidance do you need and want from God?

Phase 10: Praise. Adore and admire God. Compliment him. Praise him for who he is and thank him for what he has done.

ENDNOTES

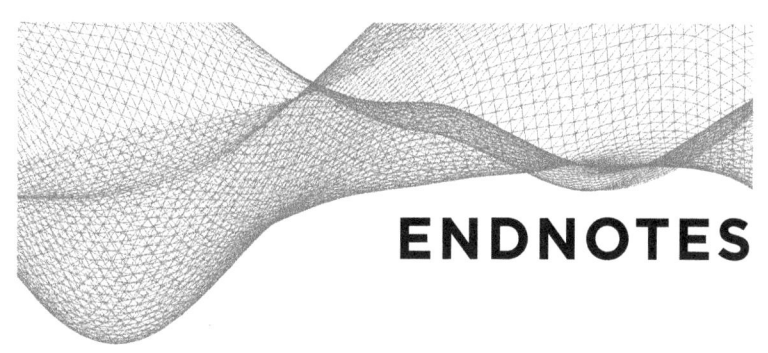

1   See "BIRSt Launch, 'On Air' with a Fresh Range of Programmes," n.d., accessed February 6, 2023, http://media.bournemouth.ac.uk/about/news/jan6/contentonly_1_1391_1391.html.

2   Séan Street, *The Sound of a Room: Memory and the Auditory Presence of Place* (New York: Routledge, 2020), 64.

3   https://www.films.com/id/9339/Arthur_Miller_An_Interview.htm, 00:27:25

4   "Mysterious Ancient Temples Resonate at the 'Holy Frequency'," *Interesting Engineering*, December 1, 2016, https://interestingengineering.com/science/temples-resonates-frequency-111-hz.

5   Nataša Pantović Nuit[?], *Chanting Mantras: Guide to Chanting Mantras with Best Chords* (n.p.: Artof4elements, 2015), 10.

6   Meg Patterson, *Hooked? NET: The New Approach to Drug Care*, (Great Britain: Faber and Faber, 1986).

7   Accessed February 28, 2023, https://www.goodreads.com/quotes/457227-every-disease-is-a-musical-problem-every-cure-is-a.

8   Leonard Sweet, *Summoned to Lead* (Grand Rapids: Zondervan, 2004), 17.

9   Edwin Friedman, *A Failure of Nerve: Leadership in the Age of the Quick Fix*, rev. ed. (New York: Church Publishing, 2017), 3.

10   Joel Peterson, "Just What Are You Trying to Say?," *Forbes*, November 13, 2012, https://www.forbes.com/sites/joelpeterson/2012/11/13/just-what-are-you-trying-to-say/?sh=28cc7cc5370c.

ENDNOTES

11   TRCP Staff, "It Is Not the Critic Who Counts," Theodore Roosevelt Conservation Partnership blog, January 18, 2011, https://www.trcp.org/2011/01/18/it-is-not-the-critic-who-counts/.

12   "General Eric K. Shinseki Retires," NVC Foundation Newsletter 53, no. 7 (August_2003), https://www.nvcfoundation.org/newsletter/2003/8/general-eric-k-shinseki-retires/

13   See National Archives, "'The Buck Stops Here' Desk Sign," Harry S. Truman Library and Museum, accessed February 9, 2023, https://www.trumanlibrary.gov/education/trivia/buck-stops-here-sign.

14   See Mark W. Johnson, Clayton M. Christensen, and Henning Kagermann, "Reinventing Your Business Model," *Harvard Business Review*, December 2008, https://hbr.org/2008/12/reinventing-your-business-model.

15   The following quotations from Exodus are paraphrased.

16   See Elmer Martens, *God's Design* (Grand Rapids: Baker, 1981).

17   An exegesis of the different Greek words translated as "see" was introduced by Pastor Brent Warkentin in a message given at Ridgepoint Church, Wichita, KS. April 5, 2020.

18   Wikipedia, s.v. "music," accessed February 9, 2023, https://en.wikipedia.org/wiki/Music.

19   John Maxwell, "Are You Really Leading, or Are You Just Taking a Walk?," John C. Maxwell (blog), August 7, 2012, https://www.johnmaxwell.com/blog/are-you-really-leading-or-are-you-just-taking-a-walk/.

20   James M. Kouzes and Barry Z. Posner, *The Leadership Challenge* (San Francisco: CA. Jossey-Bass, 1987), 32.

21   The stages of leadership development are adapted from J. Robert Clinton, *The Making of a Leader* (Colorado Springs: NavPress, 1988).

22   Stephen R. Covey, *The 7 Habits of Highly Effective People* (New York: Simon & Schuster, 1989), 51.

23   David Gergen, *Eyewitness to Power* (New York: Simon & Schuster, 2001), 346.

ENDNOTES

24 Jeryl Brenner, "On the Anniversary of FDR's Birth, Read His 15 Greatest Quotes," *Parade*, January 30, 2015, https://parade.com/370879/jerylbrunner/on-the-anniversary-of-fdrs-birth-read-his-15-greatest-quotes/.

25 Dr. Sheila Litke, Kyle Faculty Lecture Series. Tabor College. 2022.

26 Max DePree, *Leadership Is an Art* (New York: Dell, 1989), 1.

27 Ilya Pozin, "16 Leadership Quotes to Inspire You to Greatness," *Forbes*, Apr 10, 2014, https://www.forbes.com/sites/ilyapozin/2014/04/10/16-leadership-quotes-to-inspire-you-to-greatness/?sh=61e3527967ad.

28 Benjamin Franklin, *Poor Richard's Almanack* (1737; Waterloo, IA: U.S.C., 1914), 57.

29 Dave Willis (@davewillis), "Show respect even to those who don't deserve it; not as a reflection of their character, but as a reflection of yours," Twitter, October 10, 2016, 1:57 p.m., https://twitter.com/davewillis/status/785554832975331329?lang=en.

30 As quoted in "No One Can Whistle a Symphony, It Takes an Orchestra to Play It," John Murphy International blog, accessed February 10, 2023, https://johnmurphyinternational.com/blog/no-one-can-whistle-a-symphony-it-takes-an-orchestra-to-play-it/.

31 Leonard Sweet, *Summoned to Lead* (Grand Rapids: Zondervan, 2004), 18.

32 "Must I Give Again?" Quoted on the website of Jerold Panas, Linzy & Partners, October 23, 2013, https://panaslinzy.com/must-i-give-again/.

33 Max DePree, *Leadership Is an Art* (New York., Dell, 1989), 11.

34 Jim Collins, *Good to Great* (New York: HarperCollins, 2001), ch 2.

35 Rick Warren (@RickWarren), "The first job of leadership is to love people. Leadership without love is manipulation," Twitter, October 22, 2014, 10:18 a.m., https://twitter.com/rickwarren/status/524942786152652801?lang=en%2010:18%20AM%2010-22-14.

ENDNOTES

36   Soundear "Types of Noise." Soundear A/S, accessed February 13, 2023, https://soundear.com/types-of-noise/,

37   A few of the assessments used to measure and develop leadership effectiveness include Myers-Briggs, Clifton Strengthfinders, DISC, the Culture Index, the Professional DynaMetric Program, Working Genius, StandOut, Leadership Personality, Enneagram, the Minnesota Multiphasic Personality Inventory, and the Leadership Personality Quiz.

38   Henry Kissinger, *Leadership: Six Studies in World Strategy* (New York: Penguin, 2022), xv.

39   Matthew uses the phrase "kingdom of heaven."

40   Author unknown.

41   Author unknown.

42   Andrew Zola, "Sound Wave," TechTarget WhatIs?.com, updated June 2022. https://www.techtarget.com/whatis/definition/sound-wave.

43   Dallas Willard, *In Search of Guidance: Developing a Conversational Relationship With God* (New York: HarperCollins, 1993), xi.

44   Marc Eliot, Paul Simon: *A Life* (Hoboken, NJ:John Wiley and Sons, 2010) 40.

45   Theodore Levitt, "Marketing Myopia," *Harvard Business Review*, July–August 2004.

46   https://www.quotespedia.org/authors/a/a-r-bernard/the-quality-of-your-thinking-determines-the-quality-of-your-life-a-r-bernard/

47   Pablo Picasso Quotes. BrainyQuote.com, BrainyMedia Inc, 2023. https://www.brainyquote.com/quotes/pablo_picasso_120309, accessed January 10, 2023.

48   George S. Patton Jr., *War as I Knew It* (1947; Boston: Houghton Mifflin, 1995), 354.

49   Walt Disney Quotes. BrainyQuote.com, BrainyMedia Inc, 2023. https://www.brainyquote.com/quotes/walt_disney_131640, accessed January 10, 2023.

50   Robert Schuller, *The Be (Happy) Attitudes* (New York: Random House, 1987) 30, 207.

51   Colin Powell, "Why Leadership Matters in the Department of State," 2003 Leadership Lecture, October 28, 2003, https://govleaders.org/powell-speech.htm.

52   Author unknown.

53   Richard J. Foster, *Prayer: Finding the Heart's True Home* (New York: HarperCollins, 1992), 157.

SCAN HERE to learn more about Invite Press, a premier publishing imprint created to invite people to a deeper faith and living relationship with Jesus Christ.

CPSIA information can be obtained
at www.ICGtesting.com
Printed in the USA
JSHW021611170523
41822JS00004B/27